Mandalas

Adult Coloring Book

By Shacream Artist

ISBN: **1519748507**
ISBN-13: **978-1519748508**

DEDICATION

This Book is dedicated to my loving parents John and Willie Mae Dorsey.
Thank you for being my rock and my inspiration.
I love you guys always,
Shacream Artist

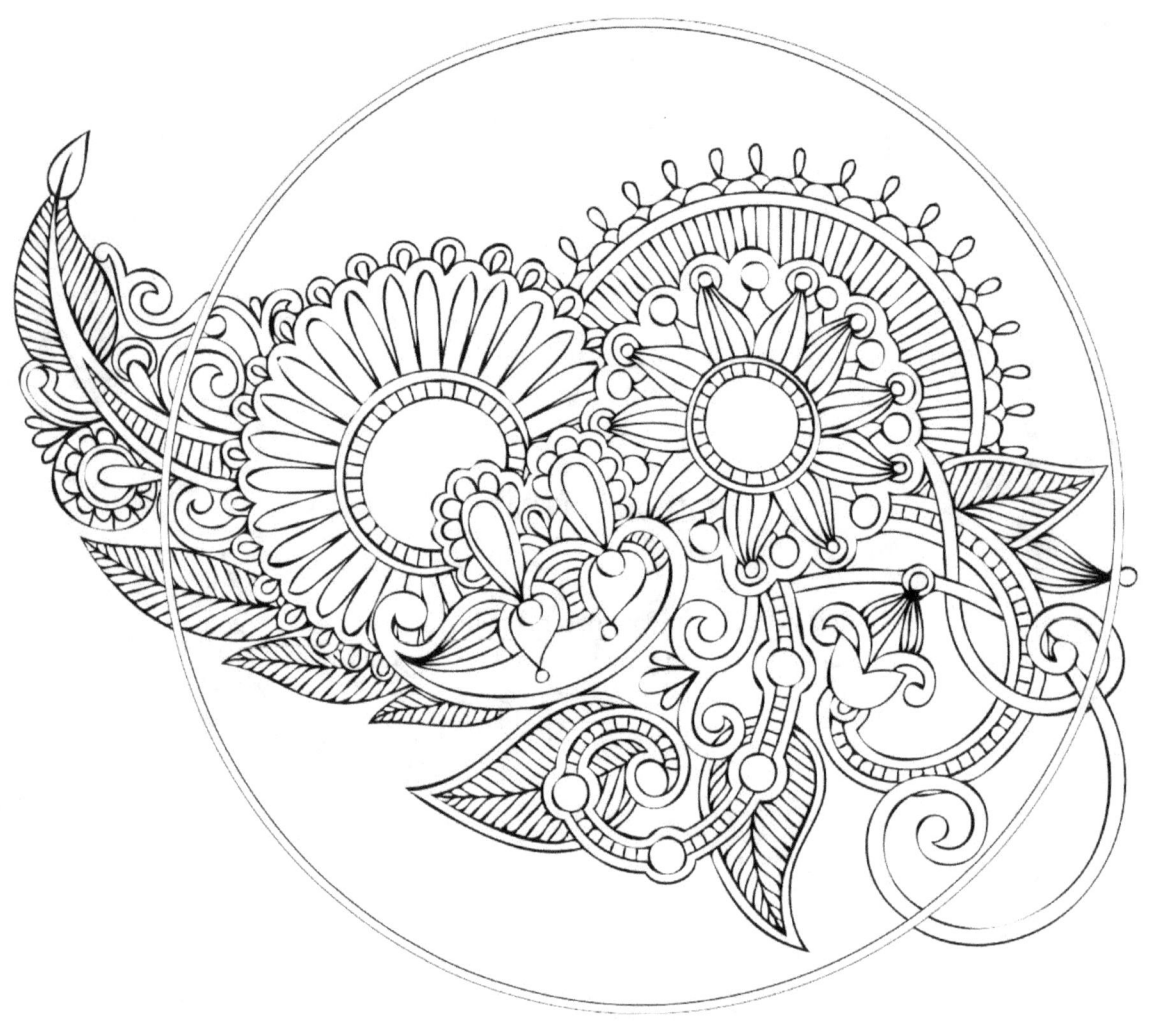

THIS BOOK BELONGS TO

_____

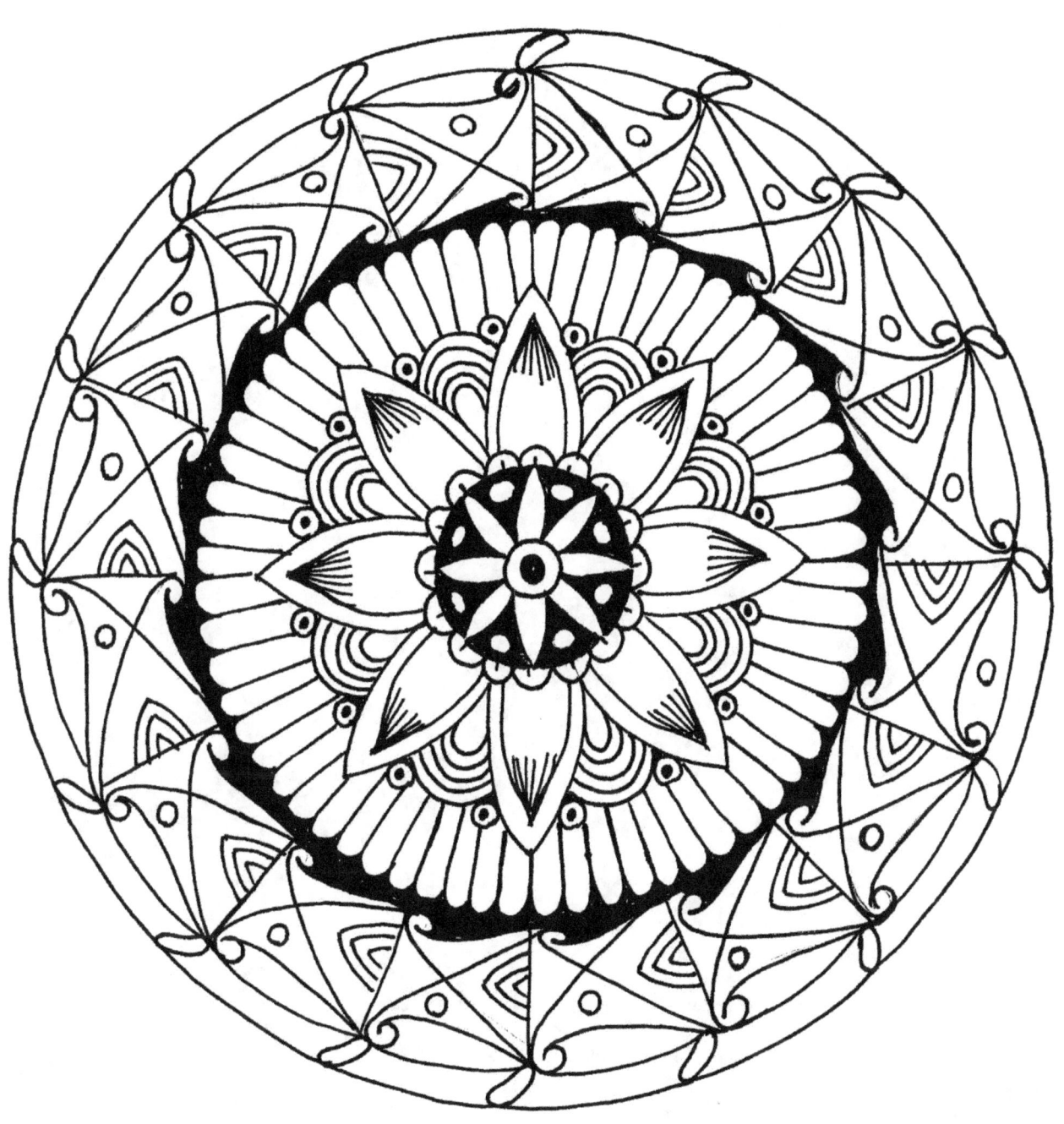

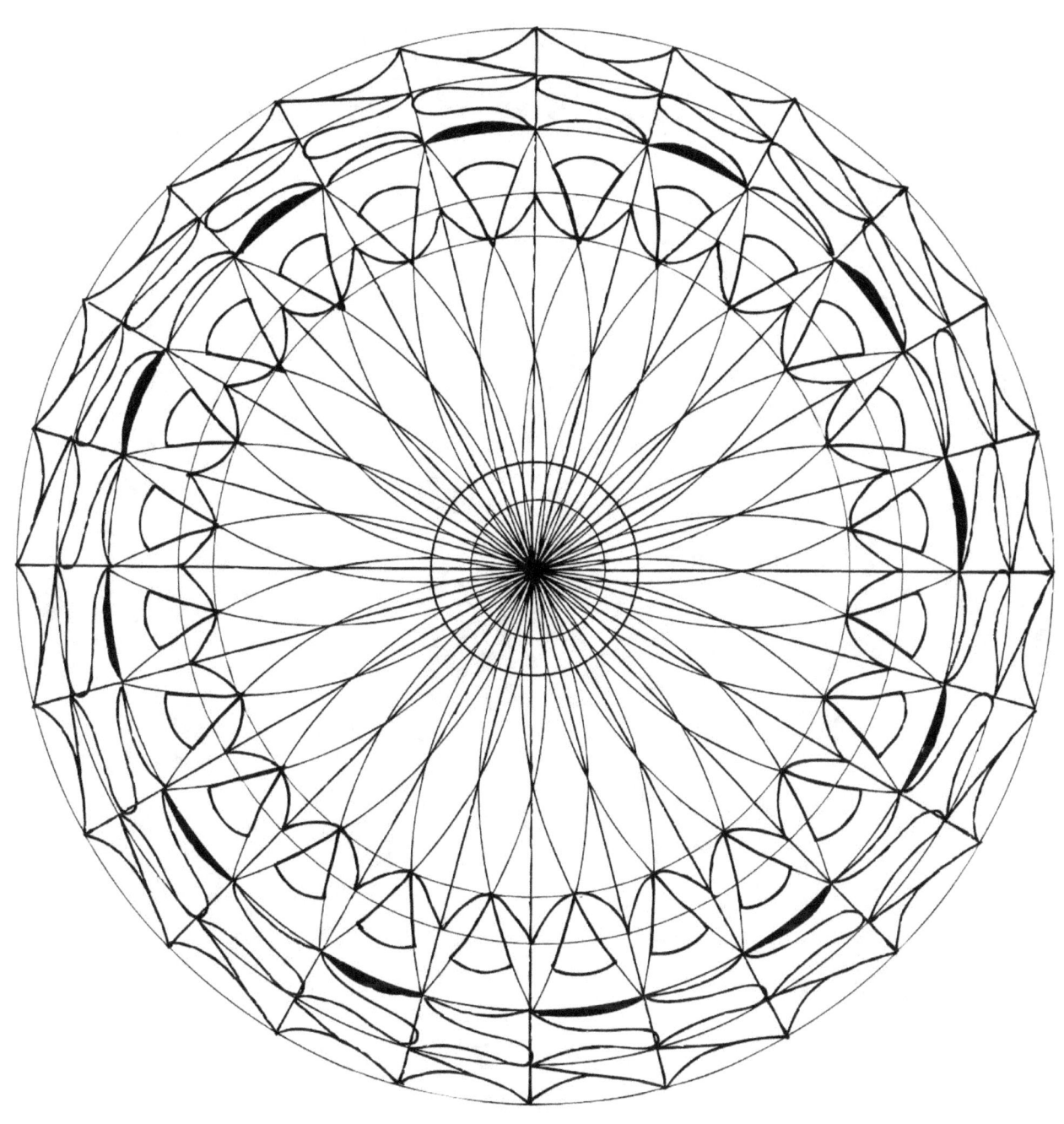

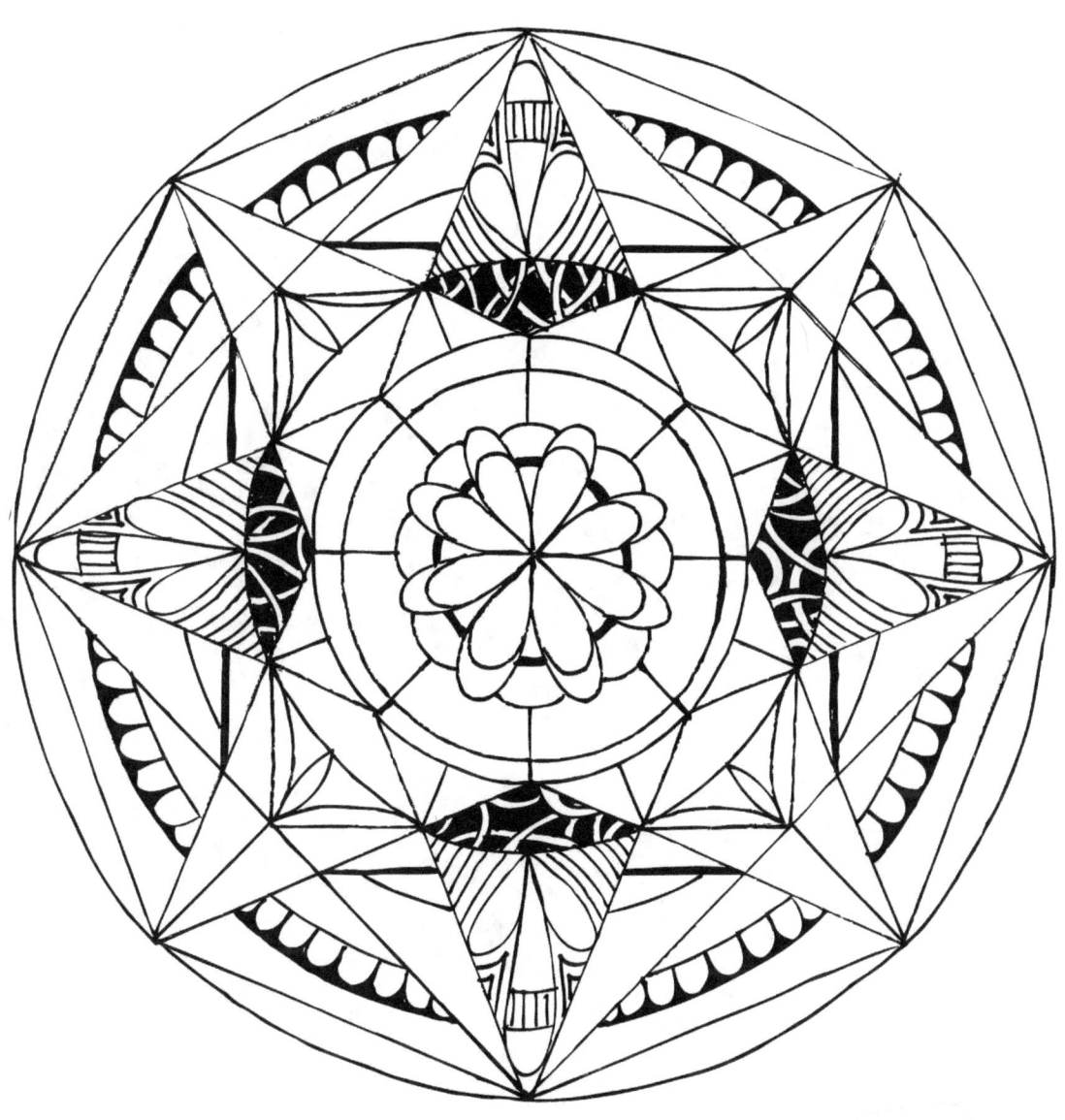

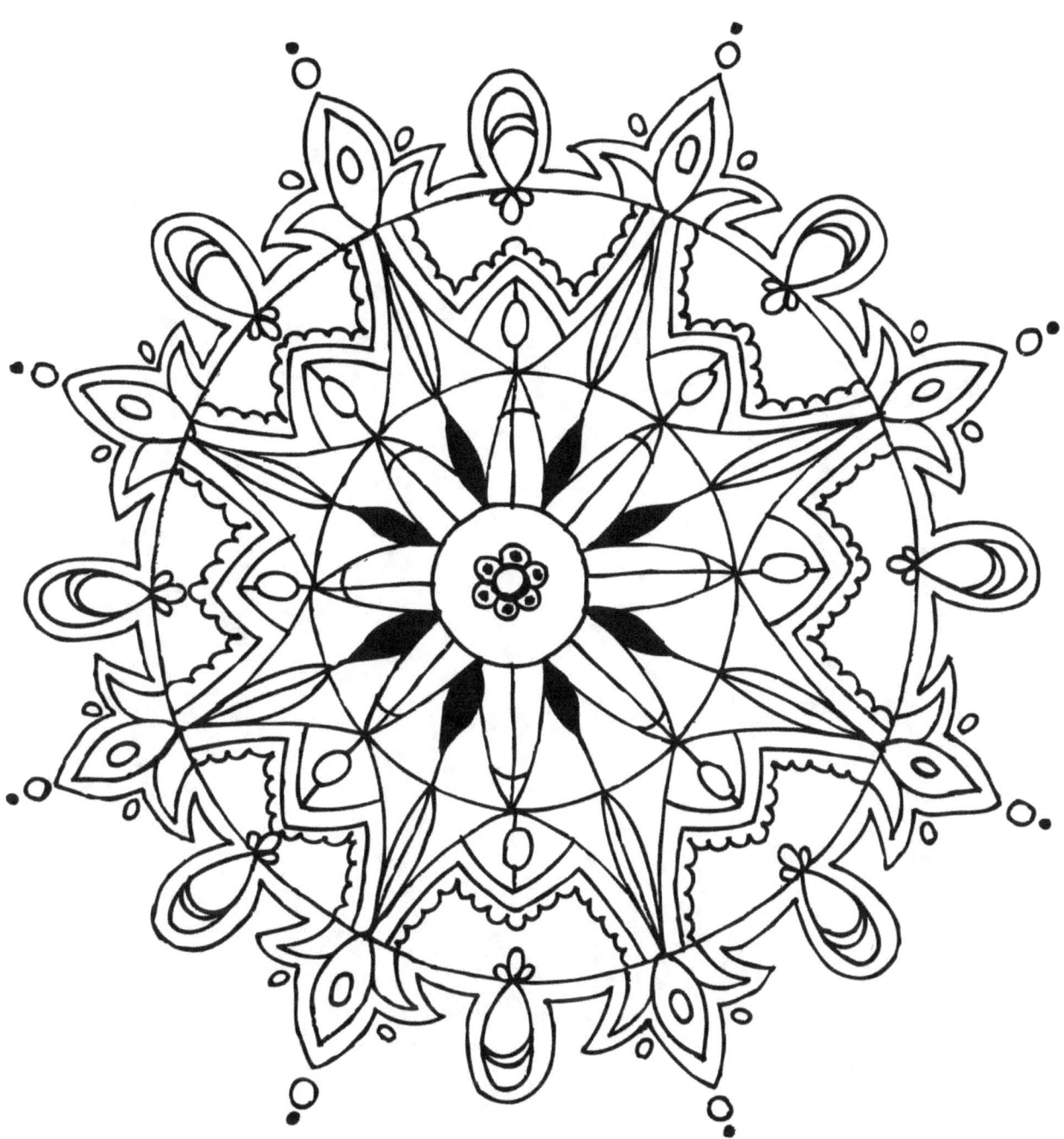

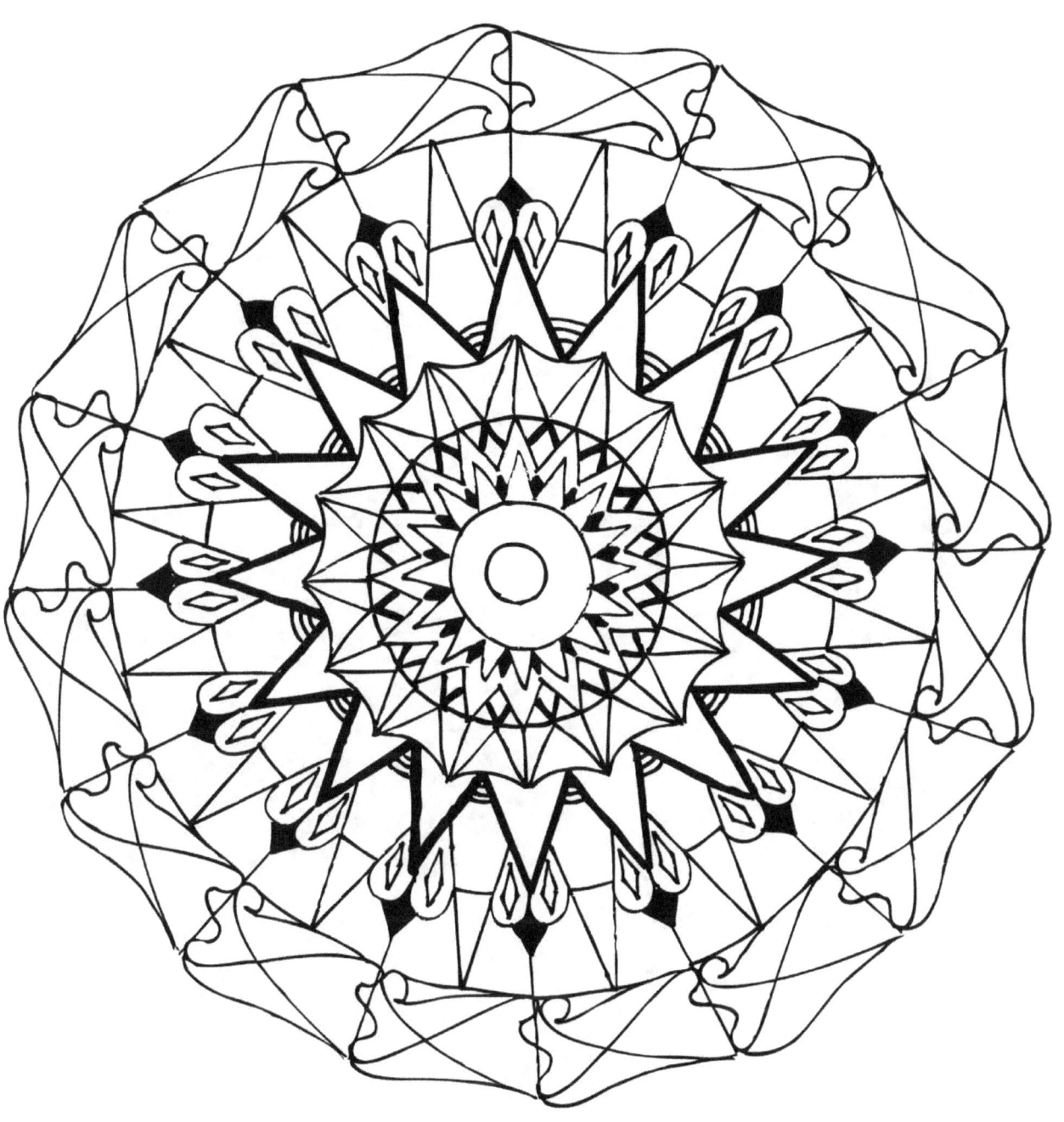

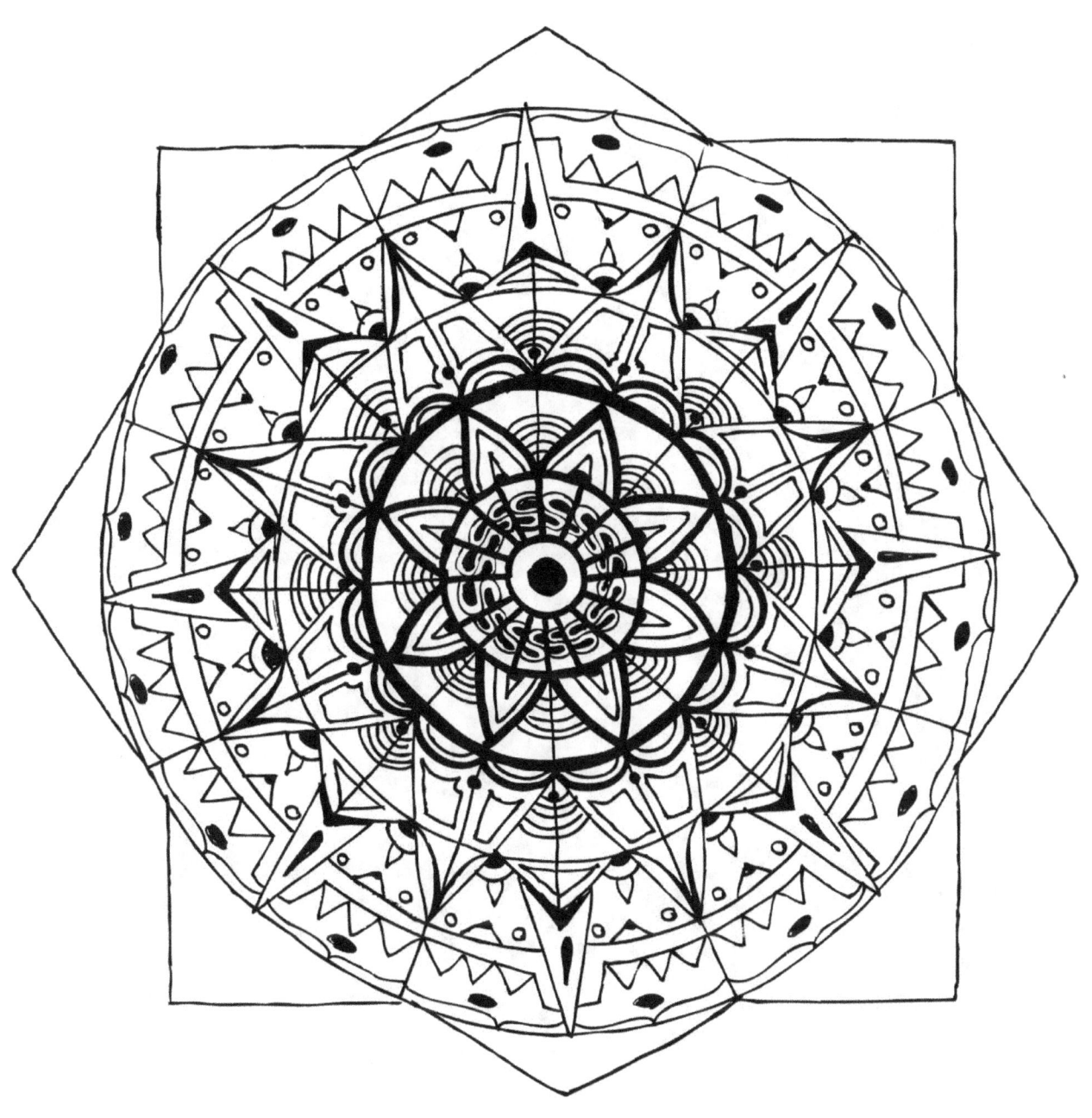

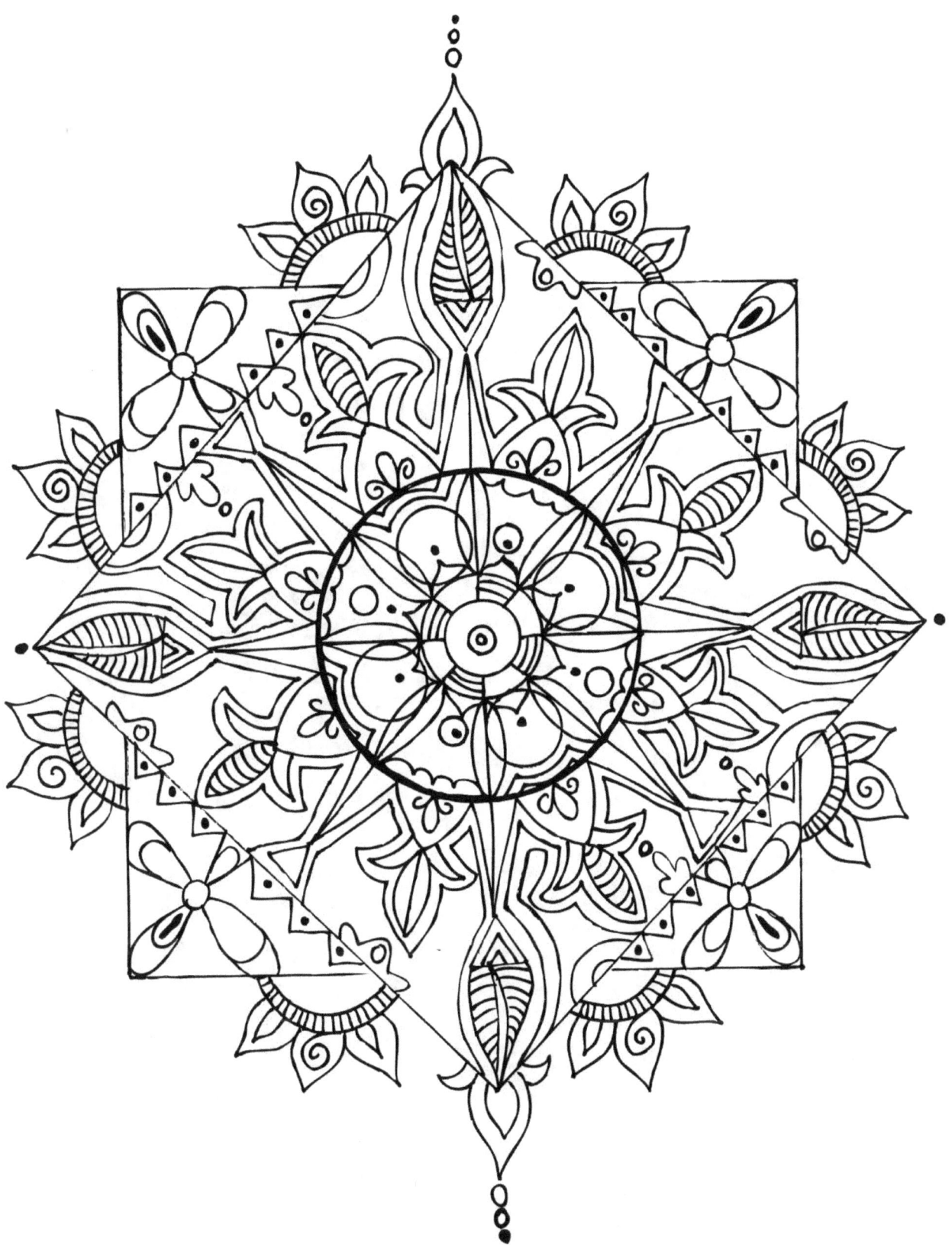

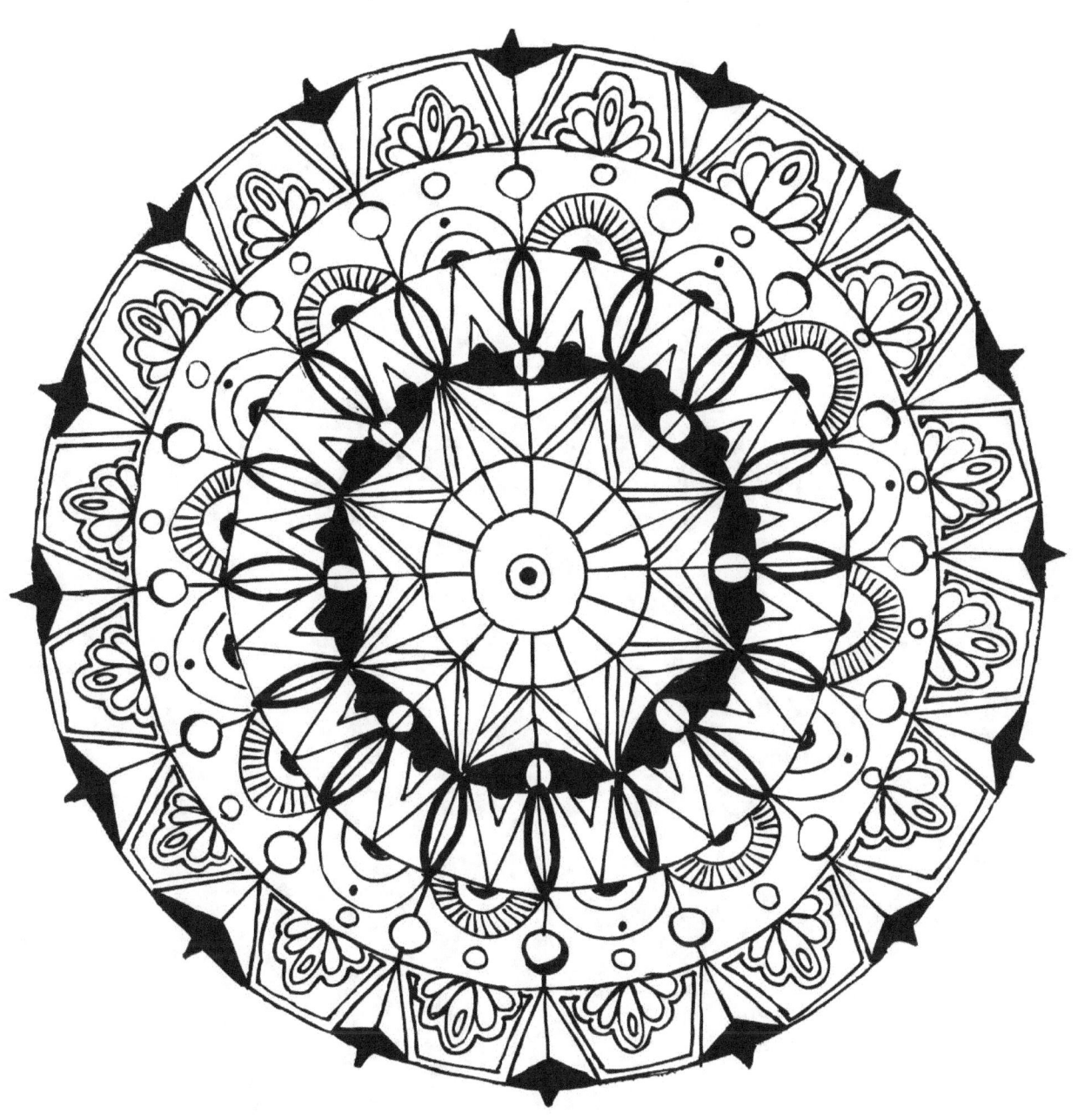

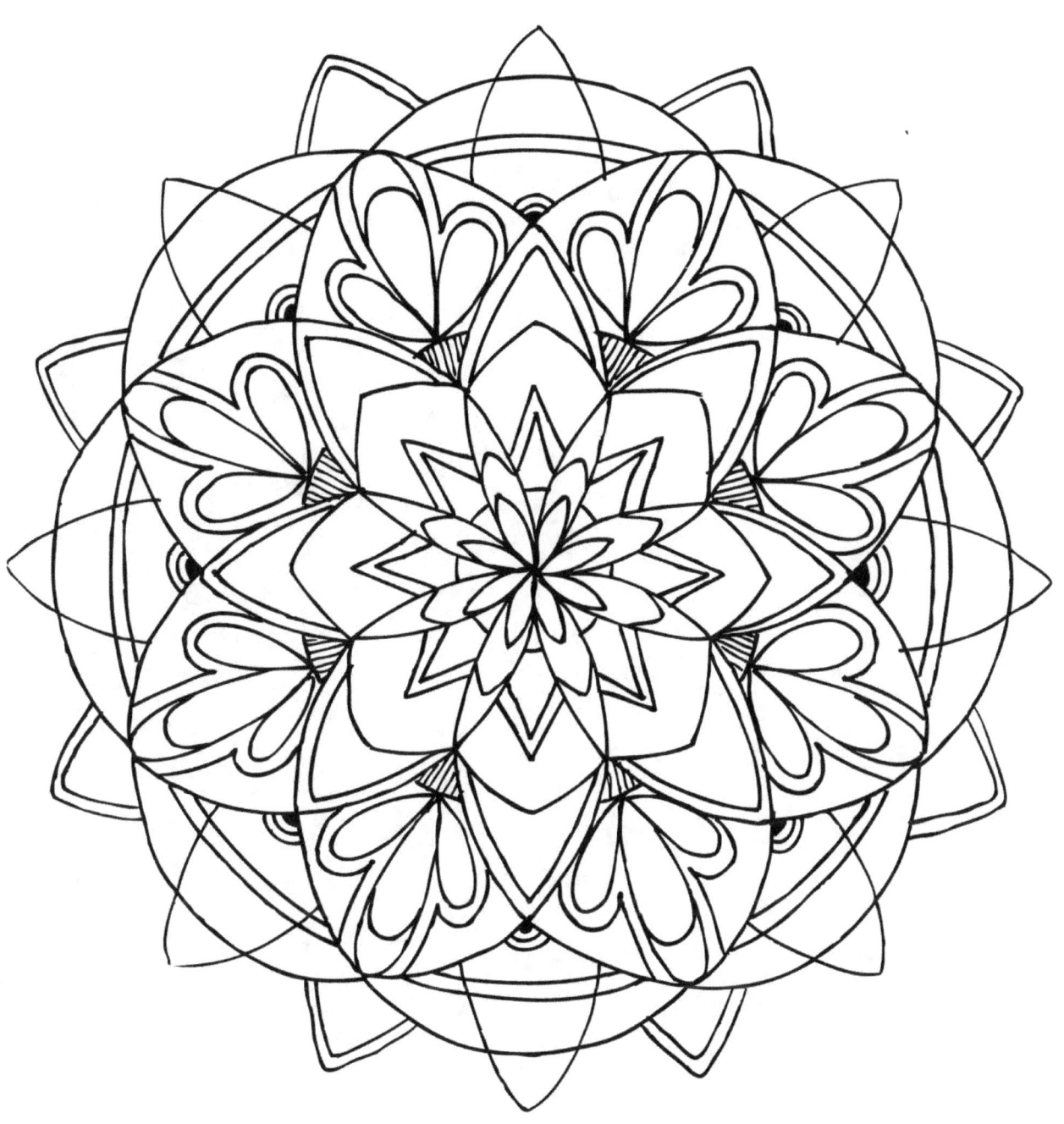

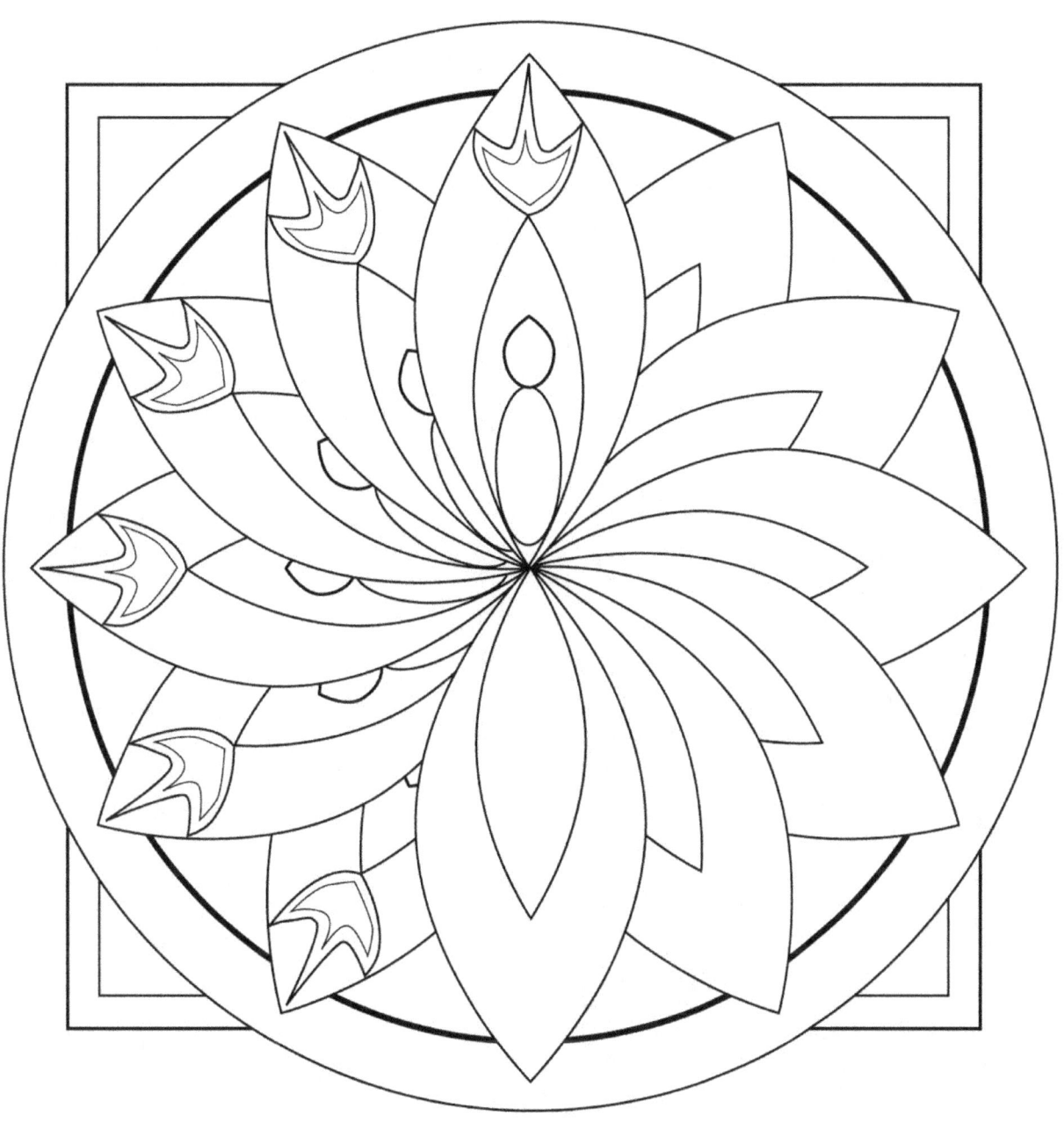

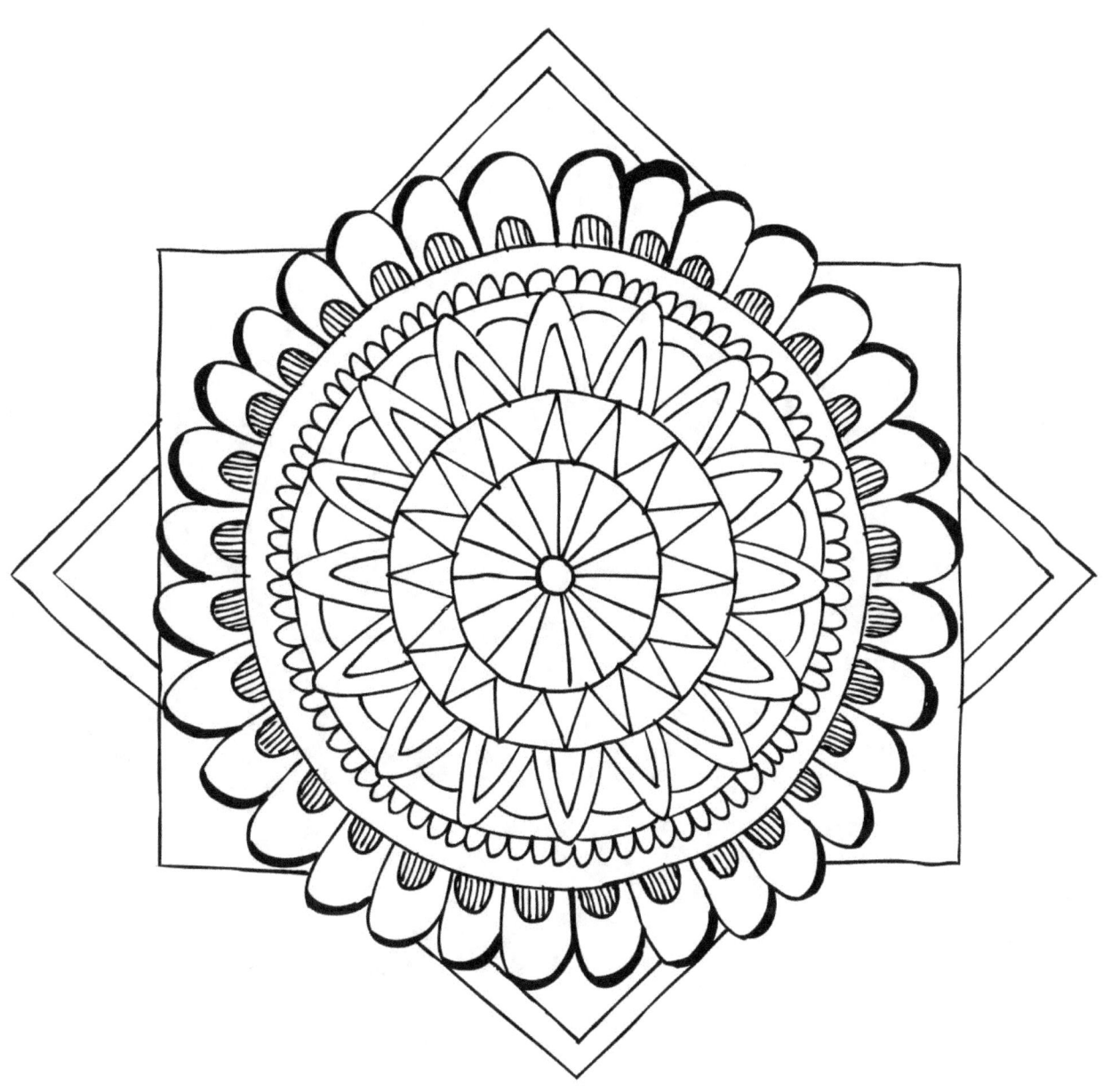

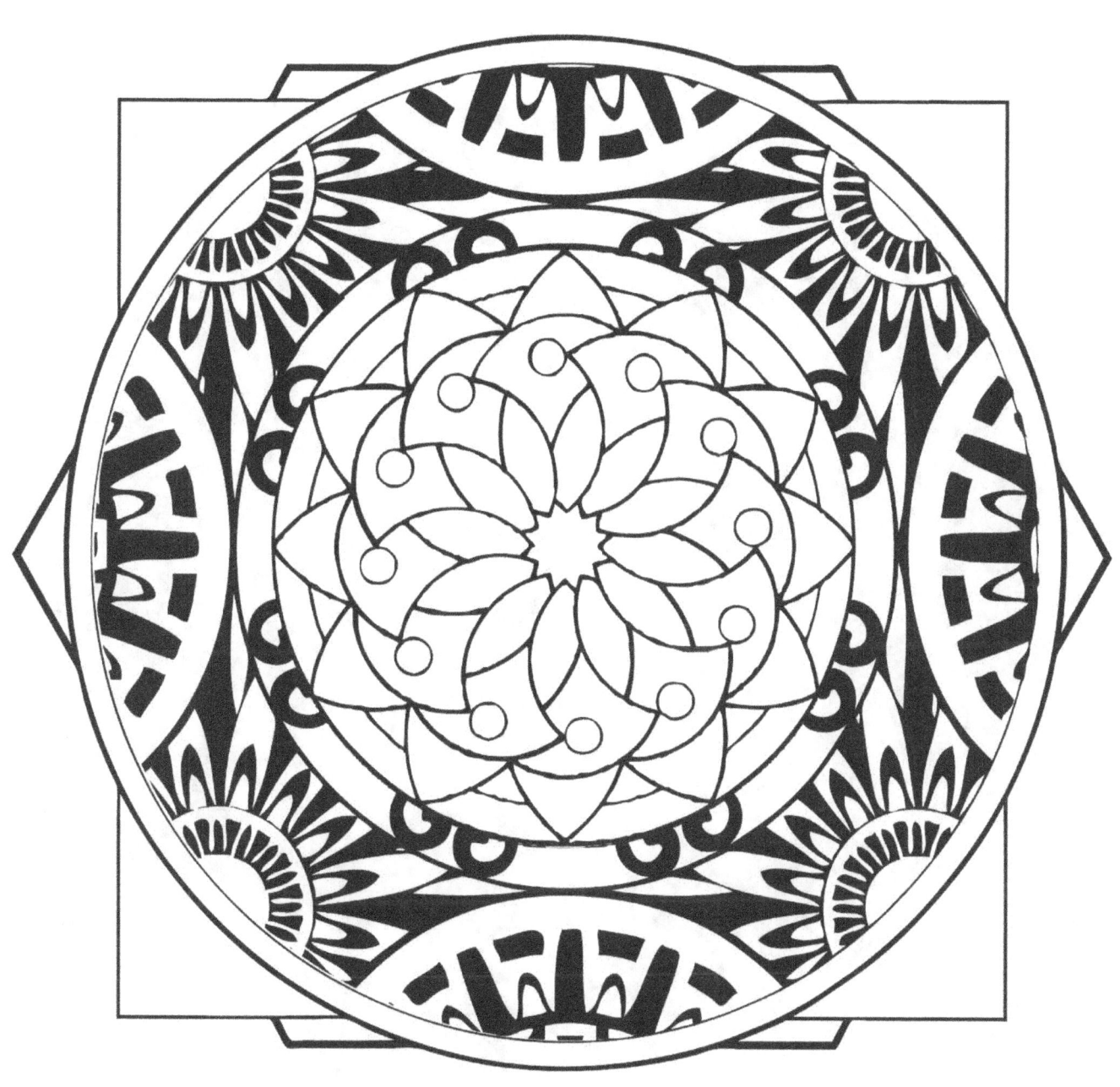

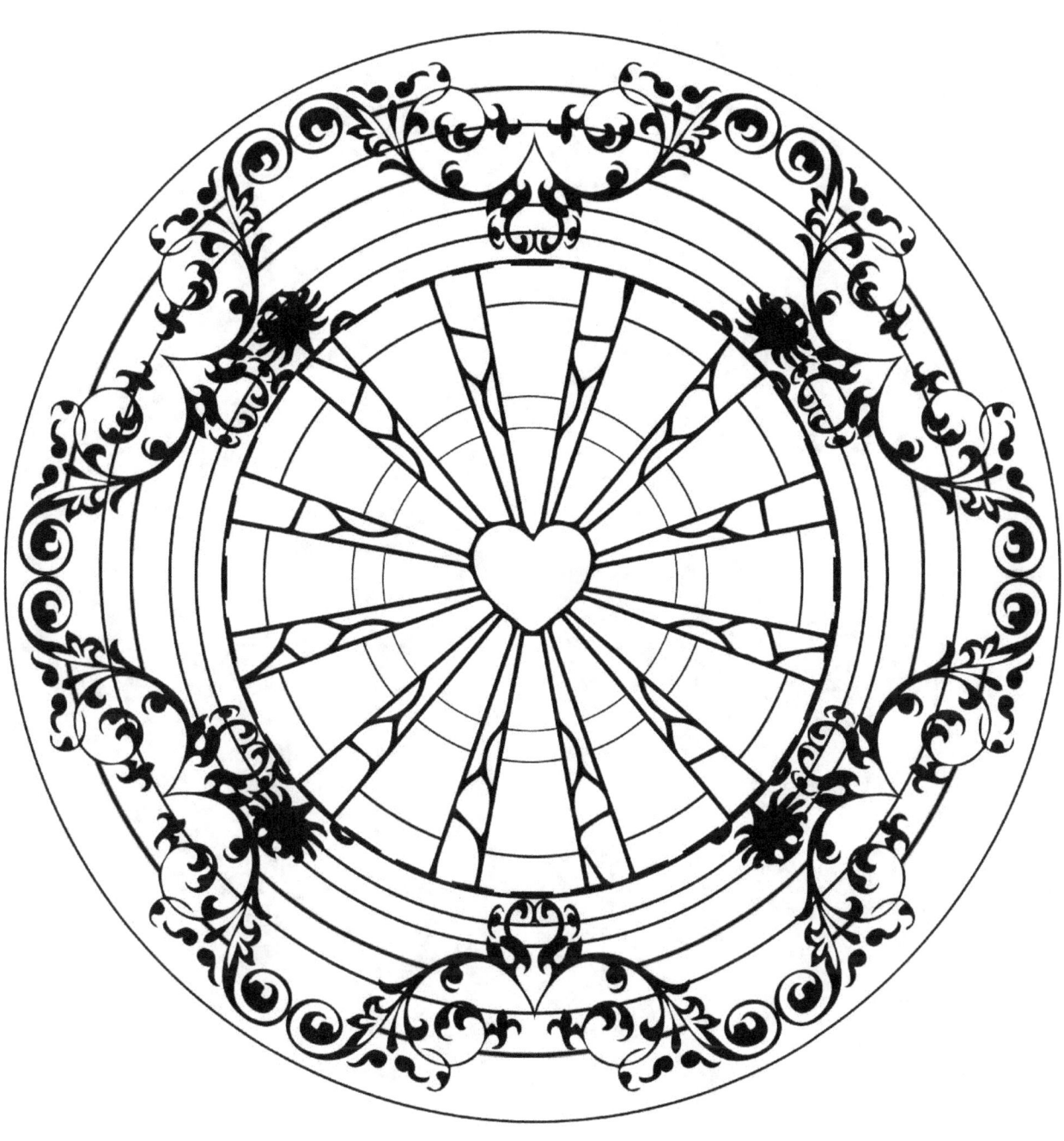

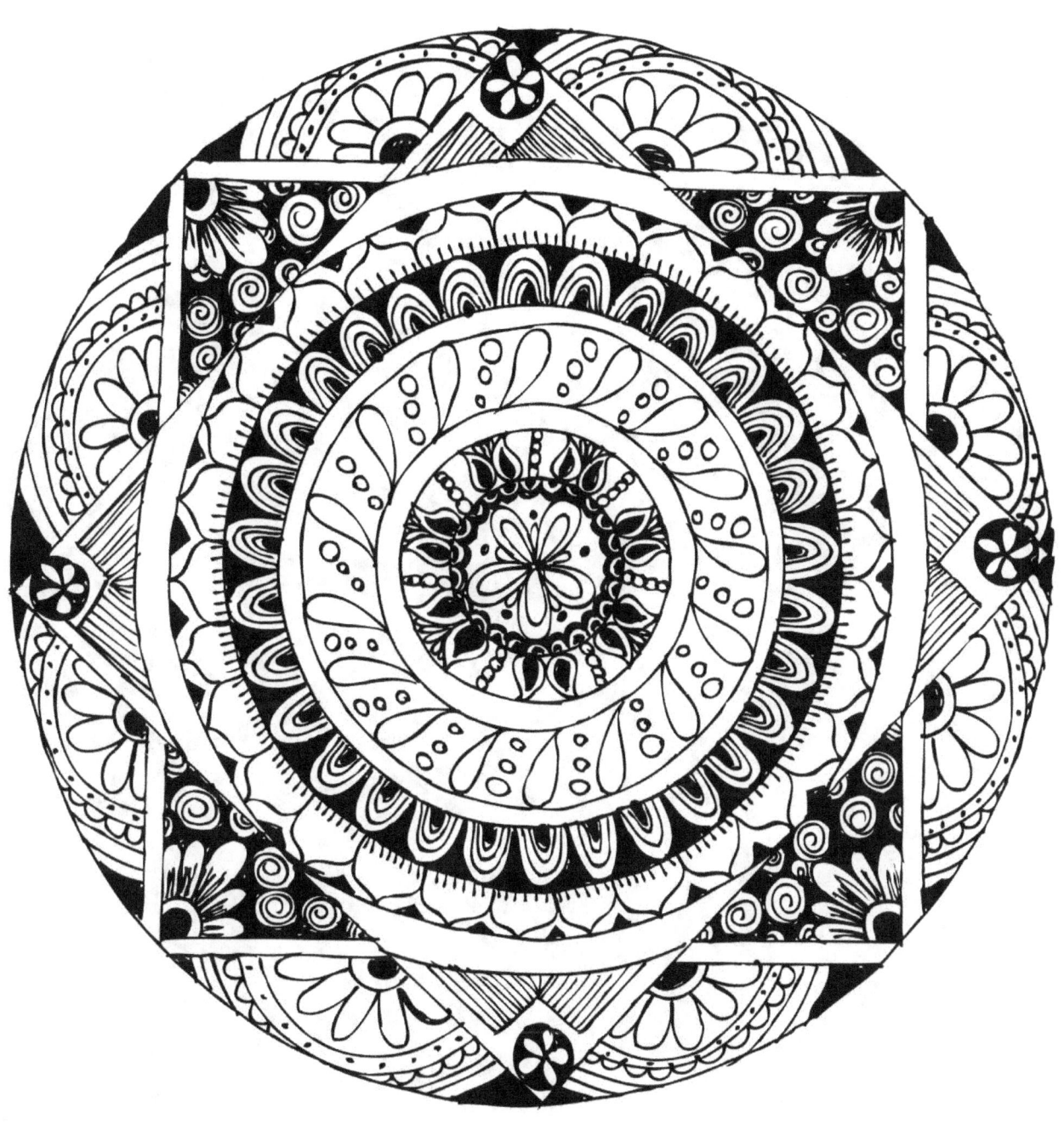

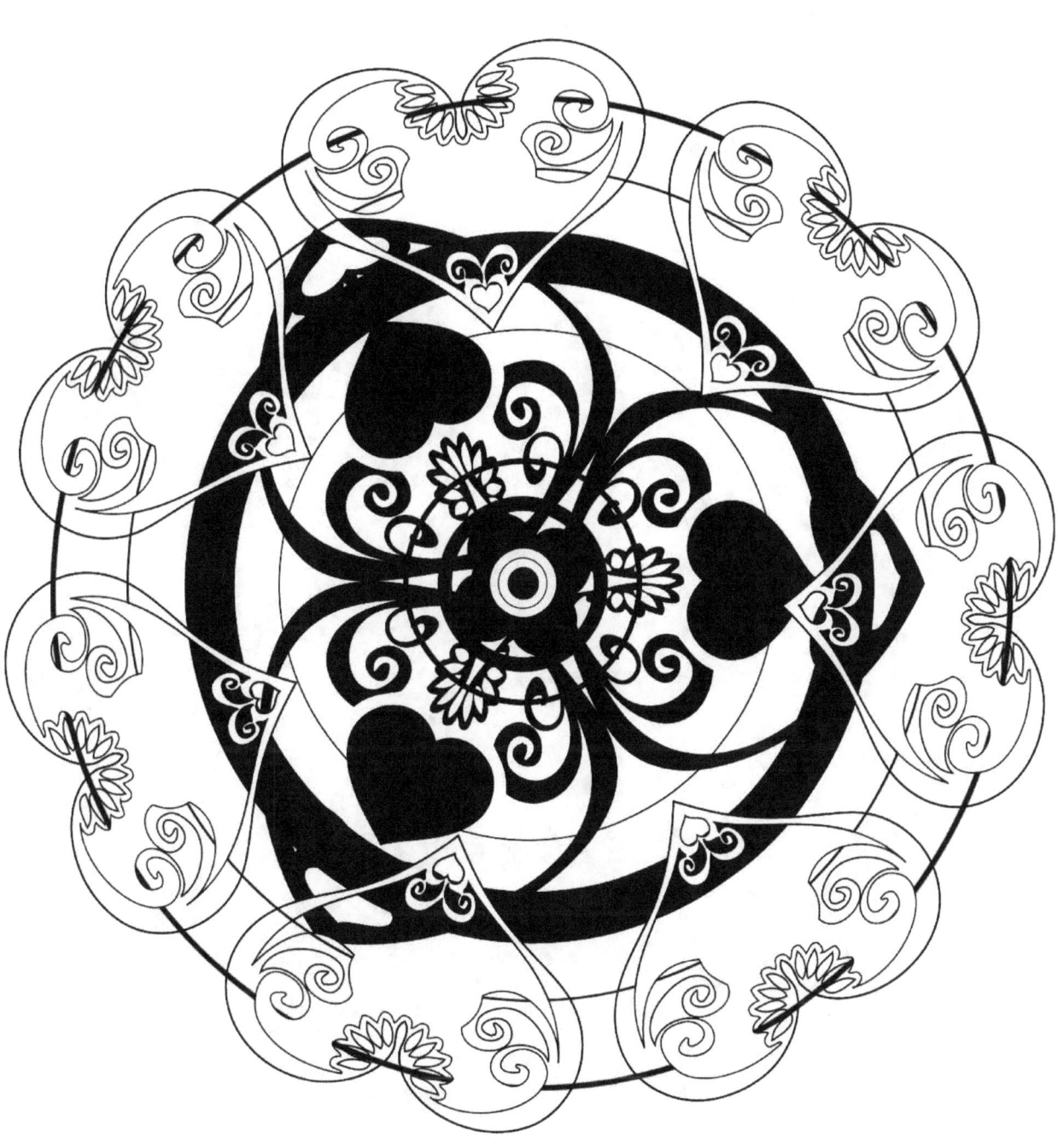

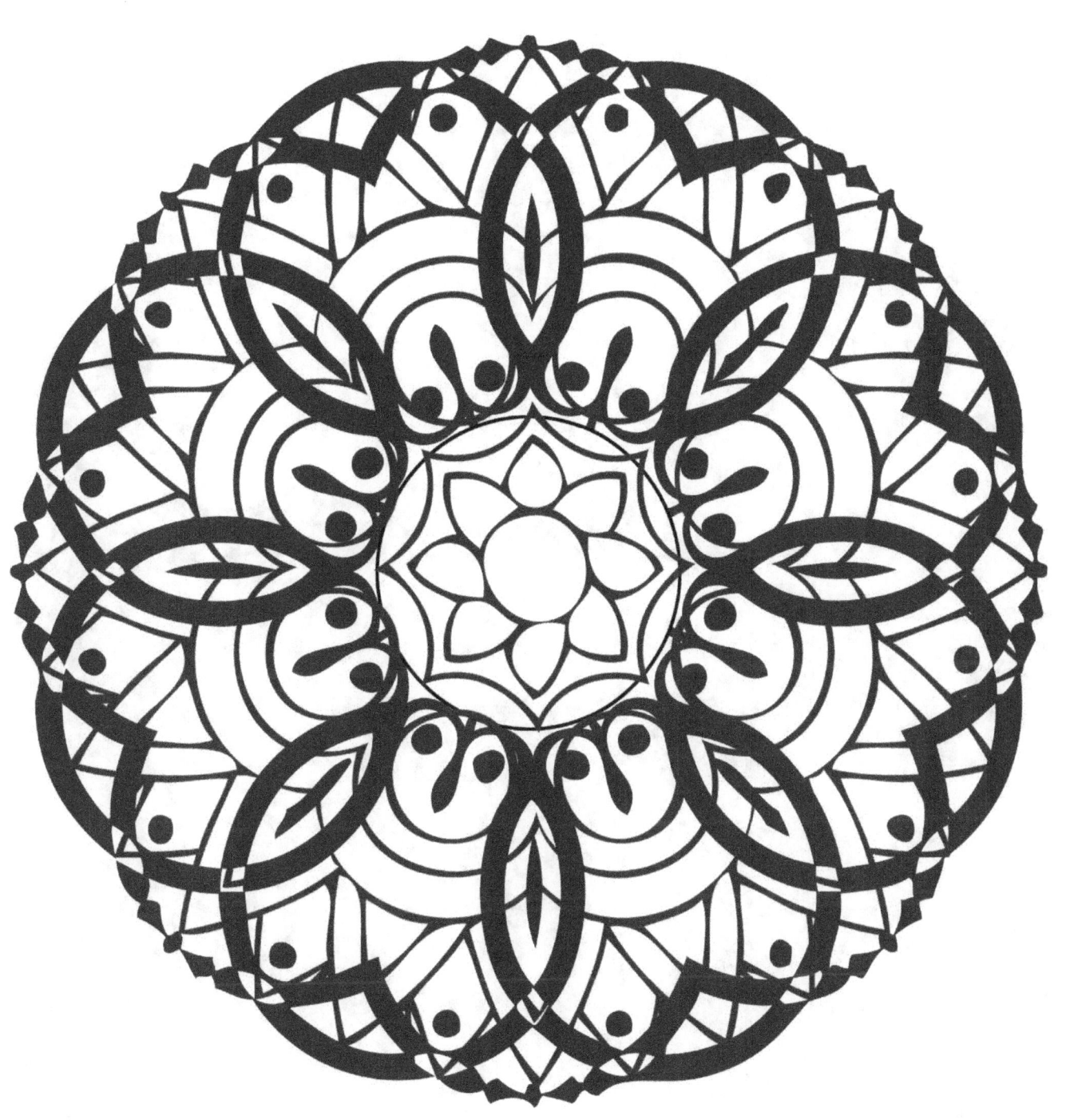

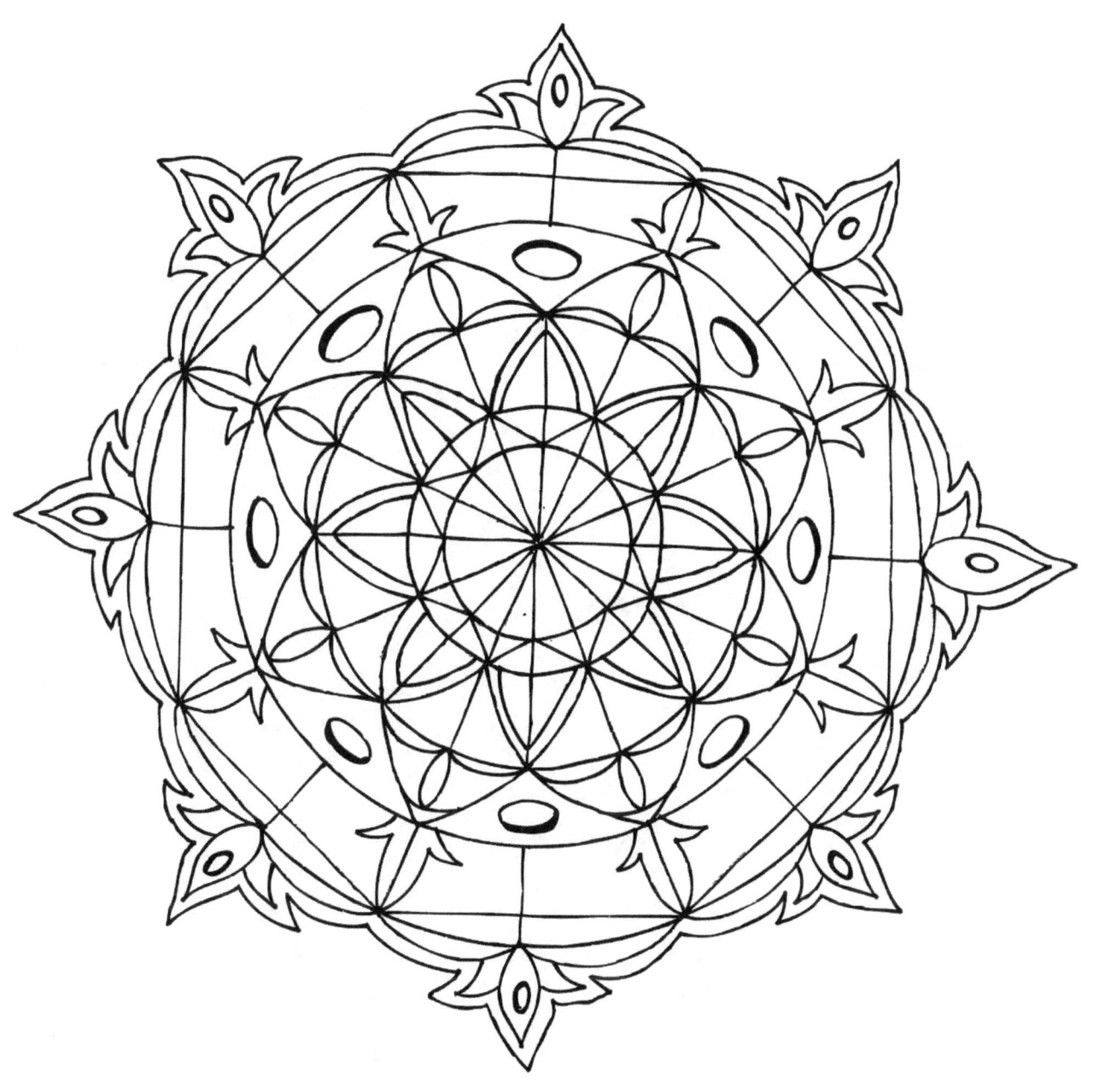

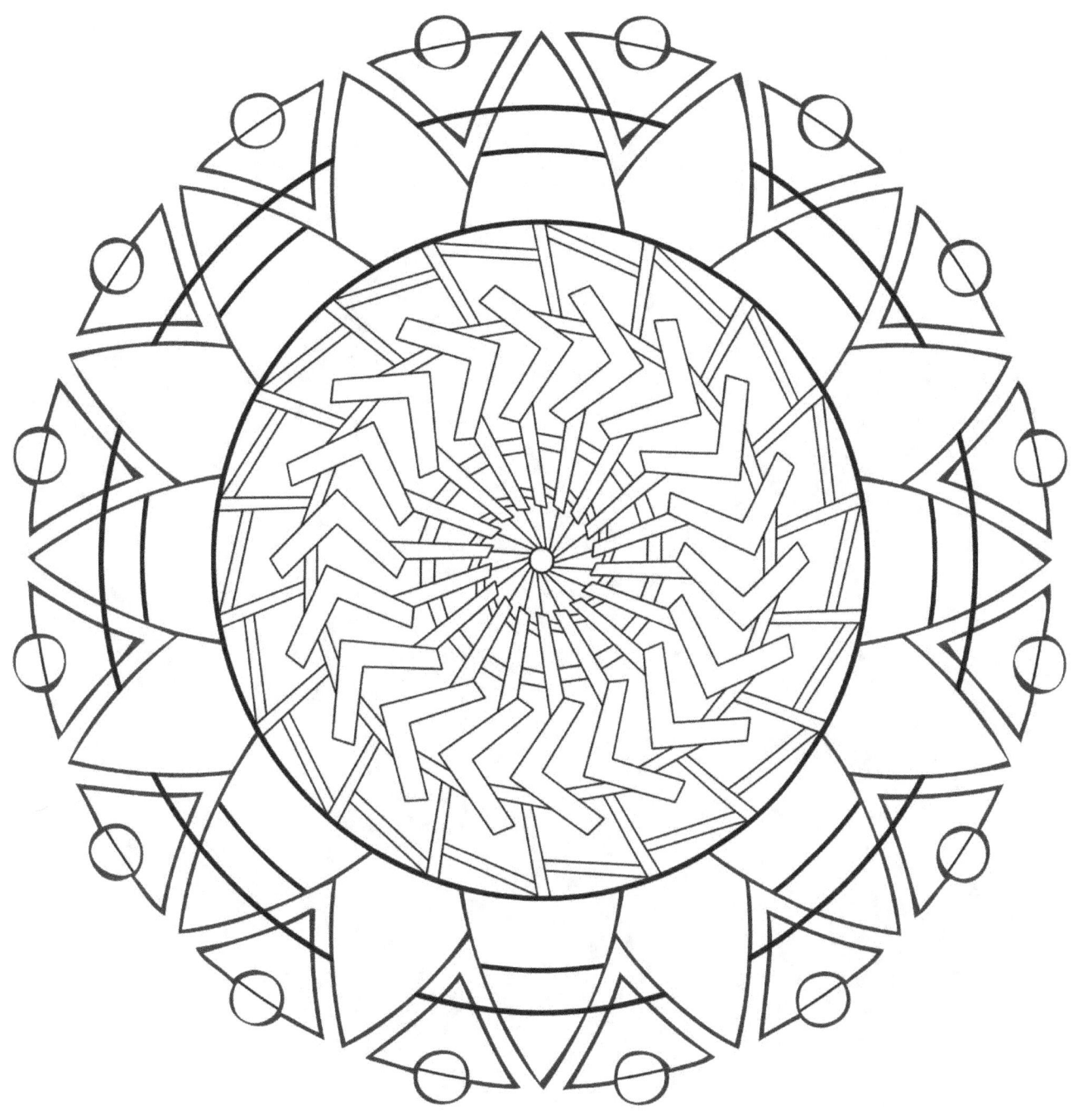

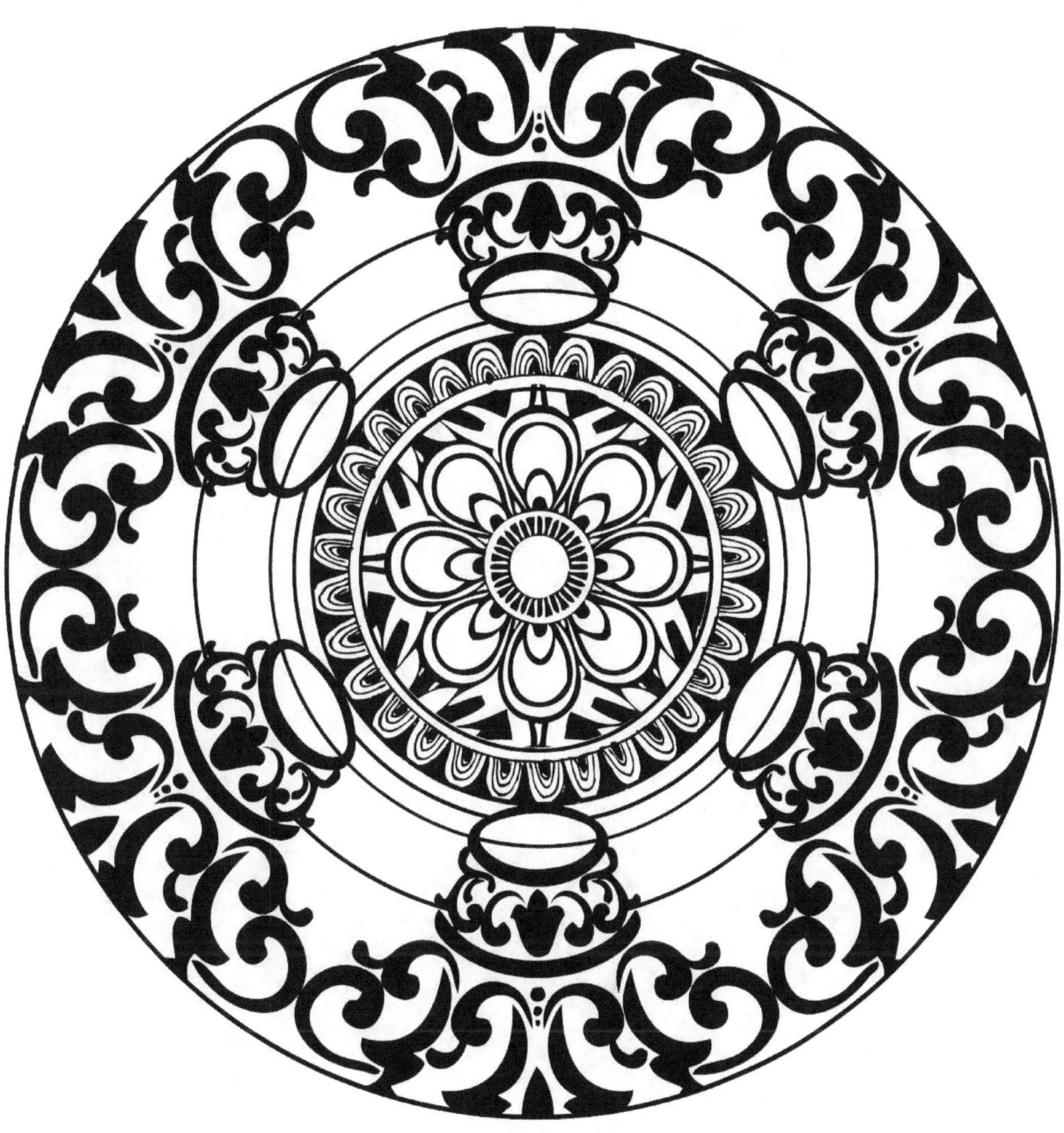

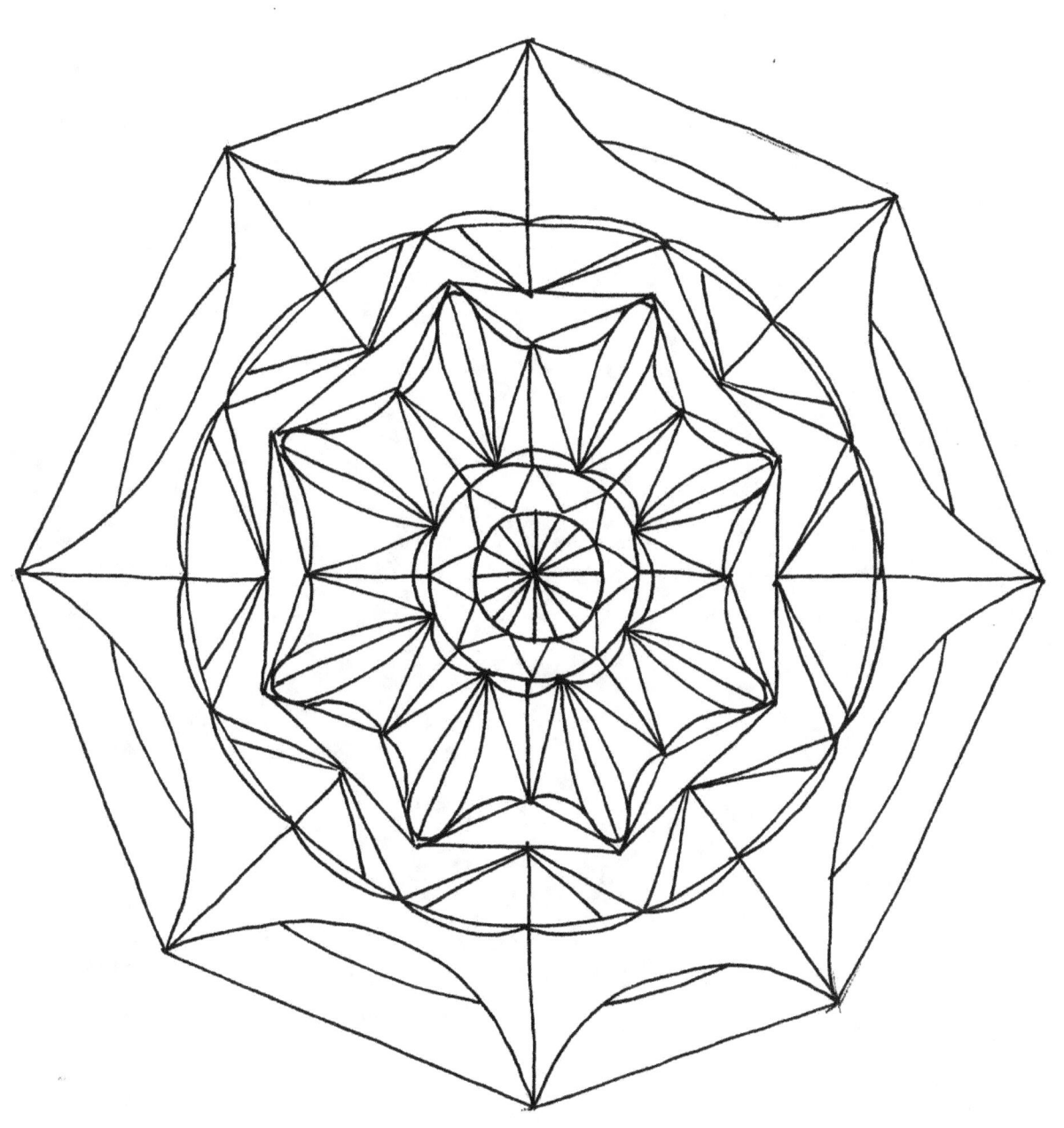

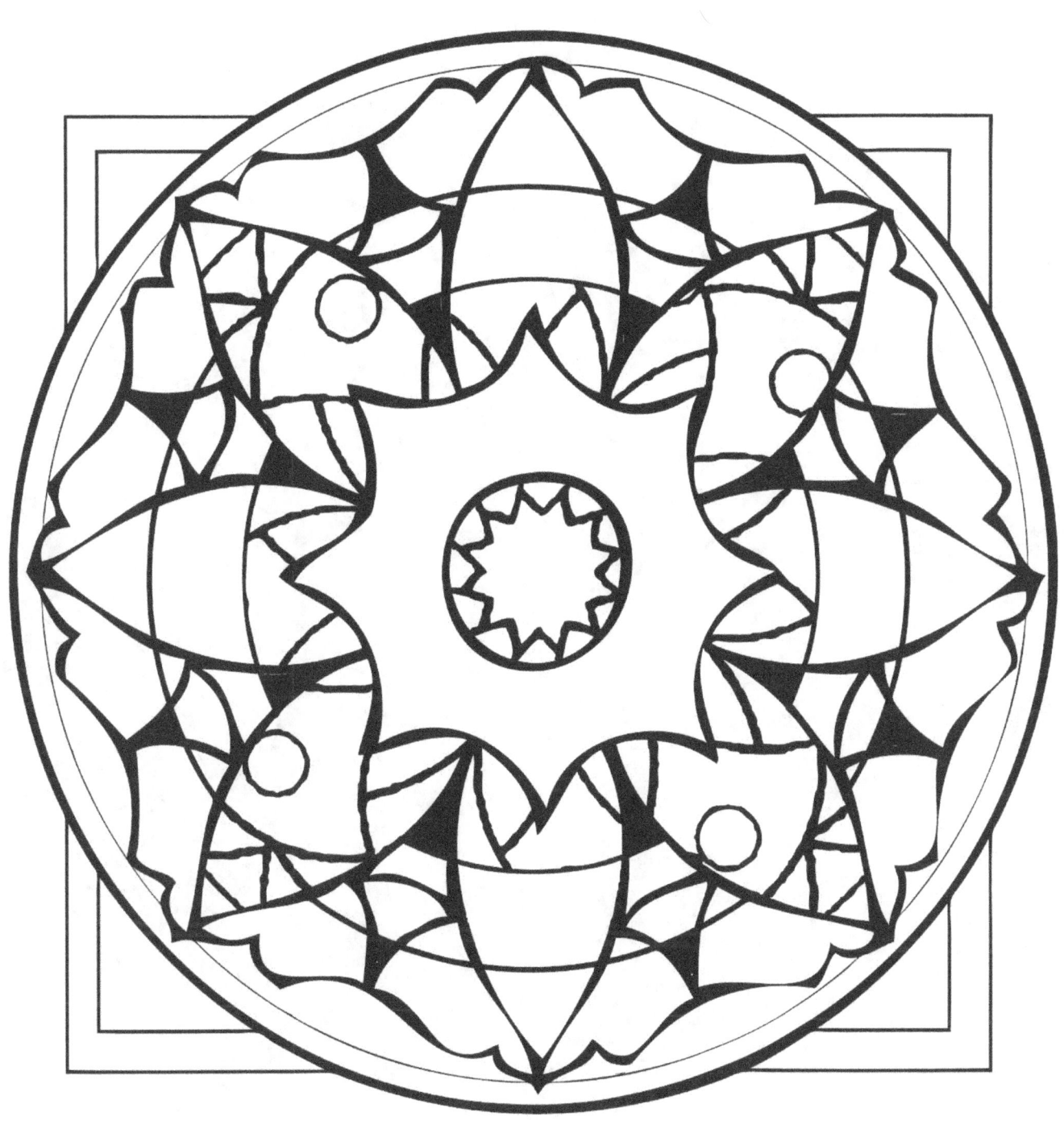

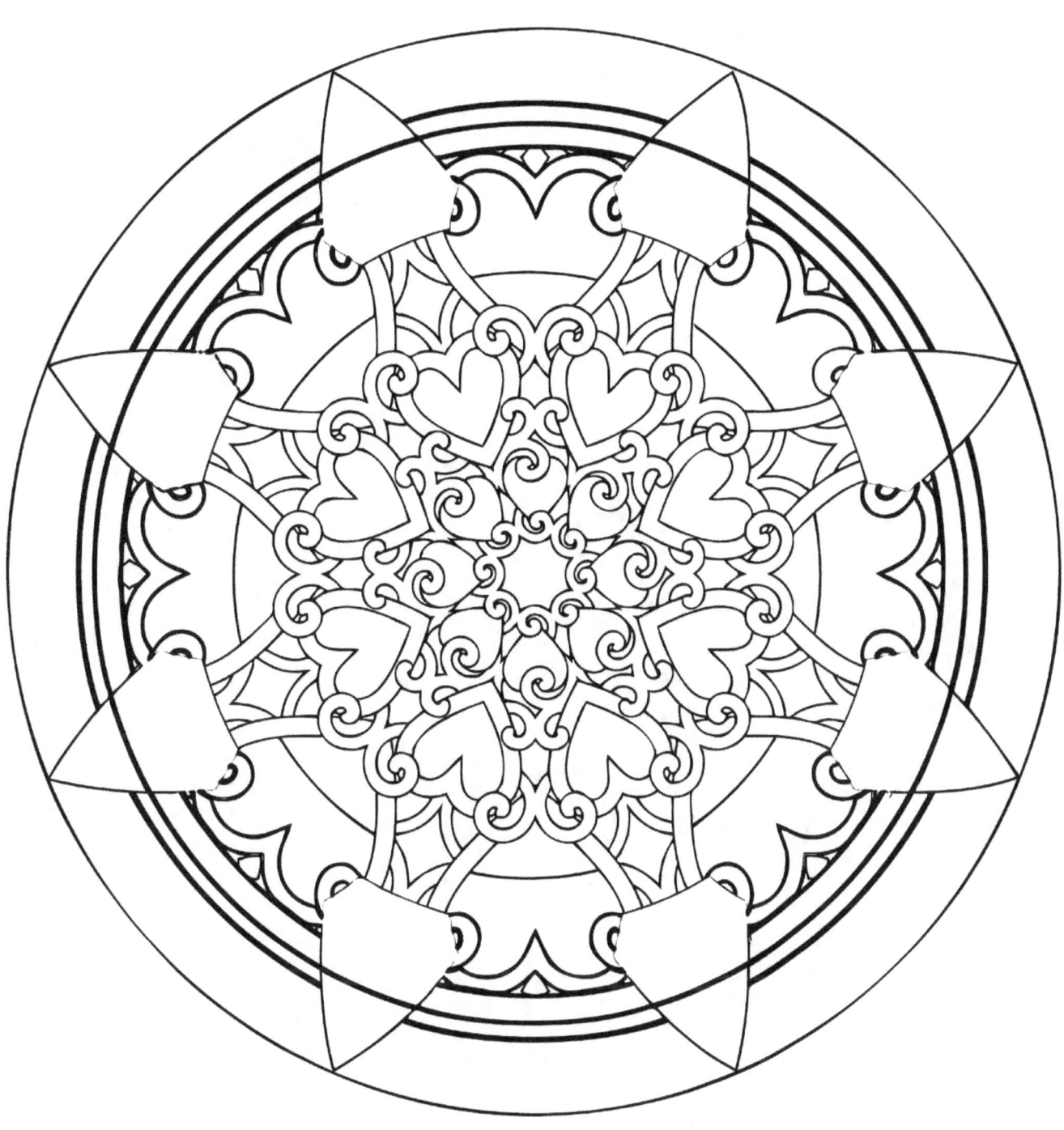

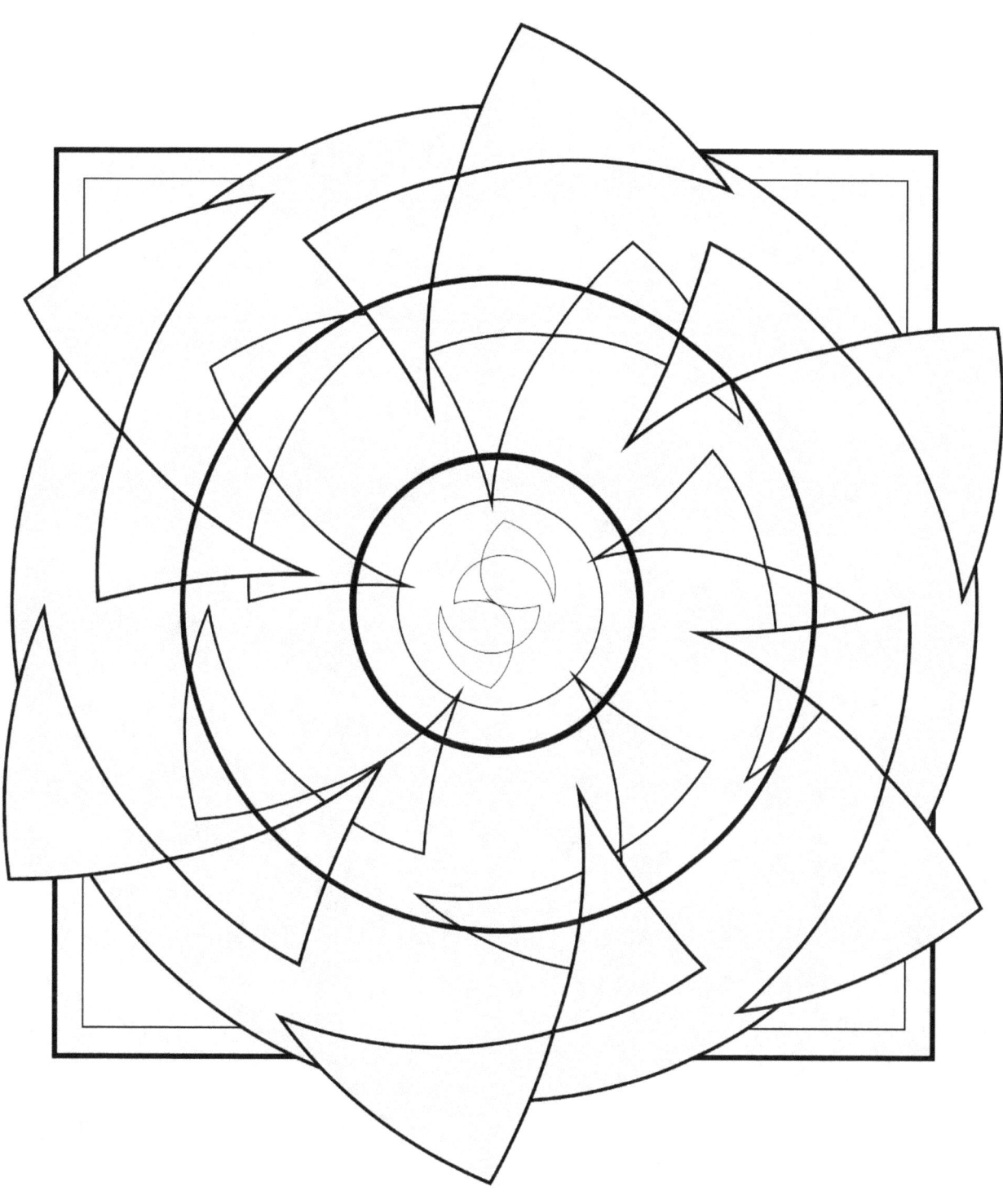

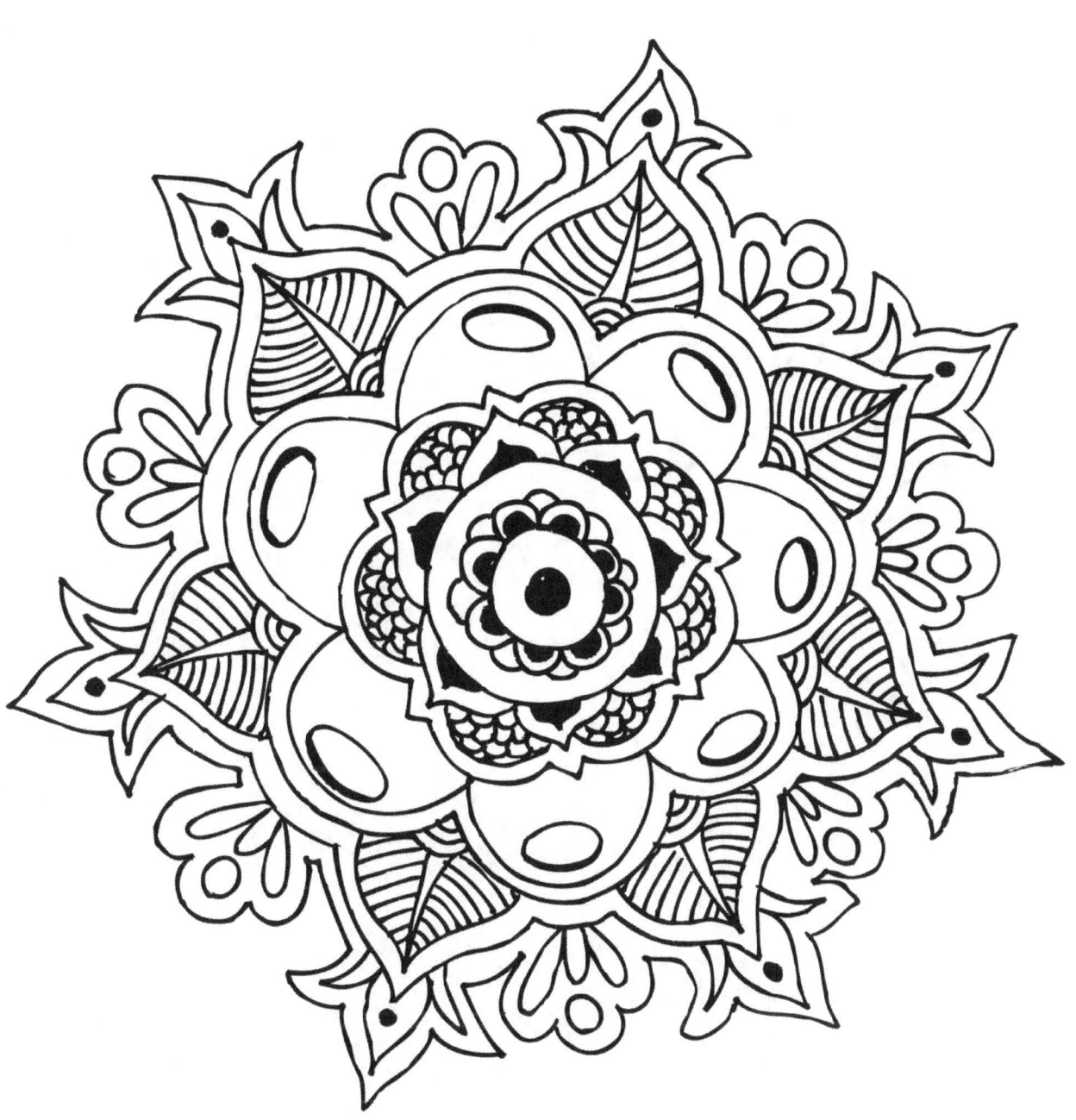

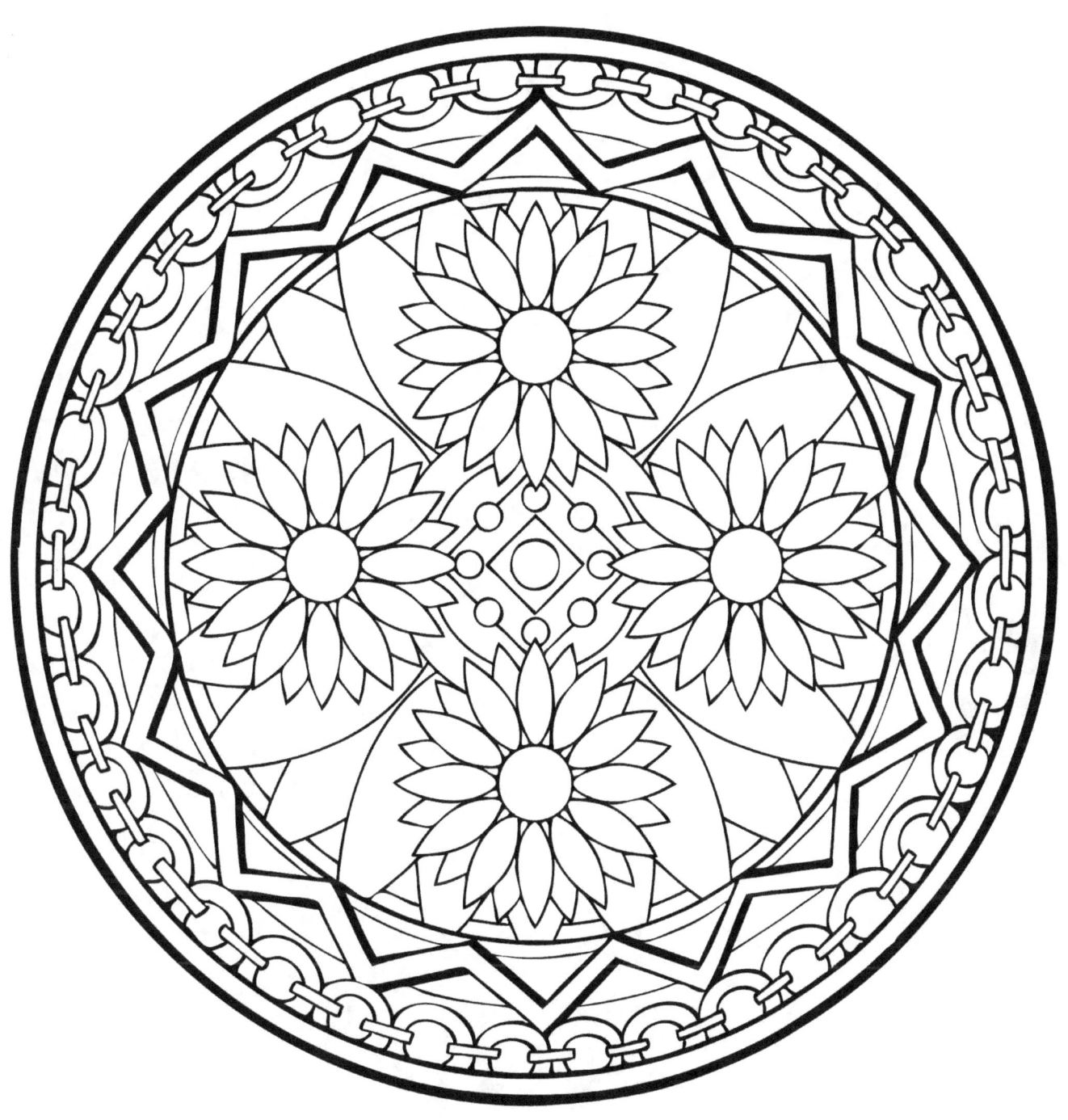

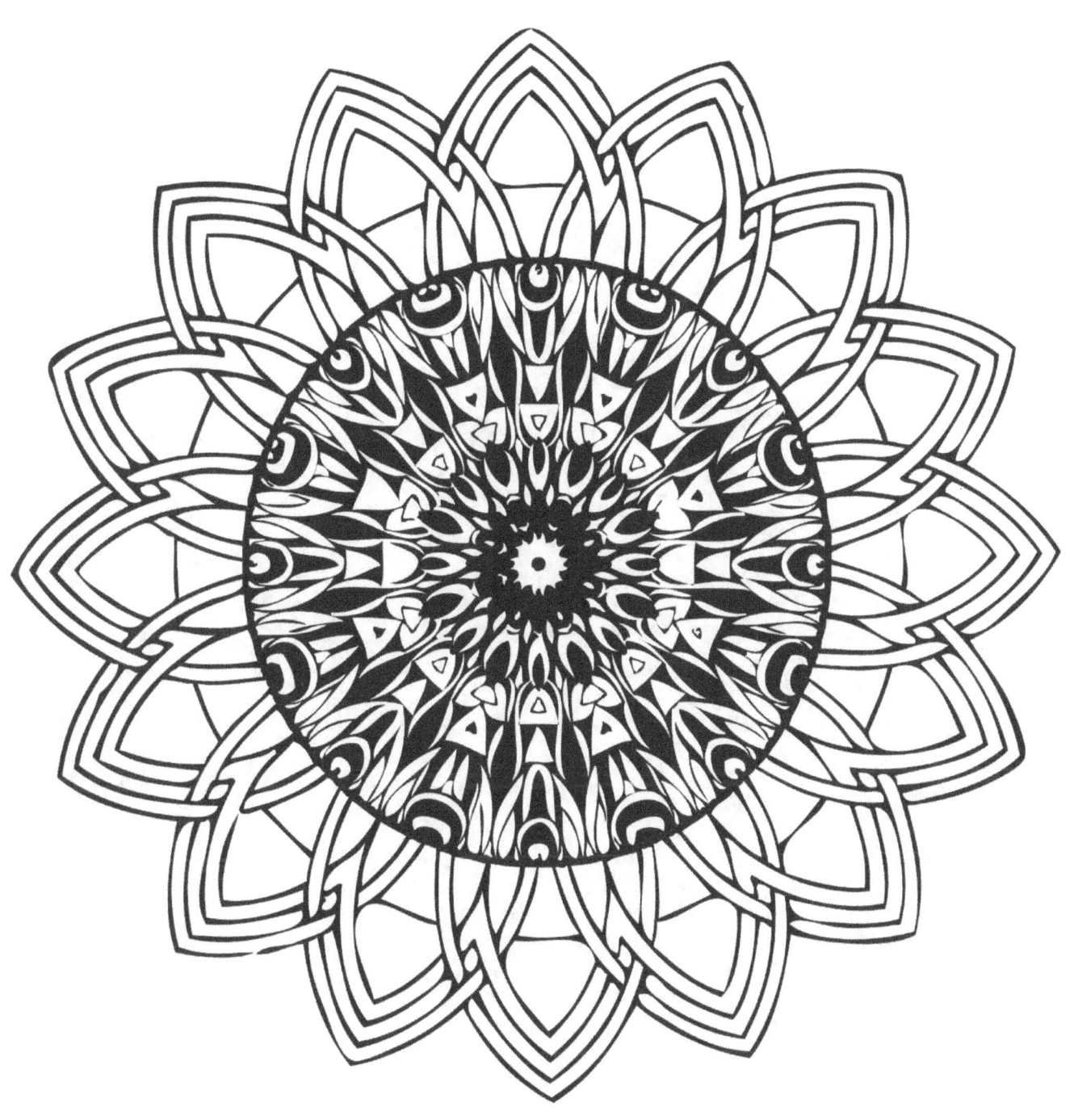

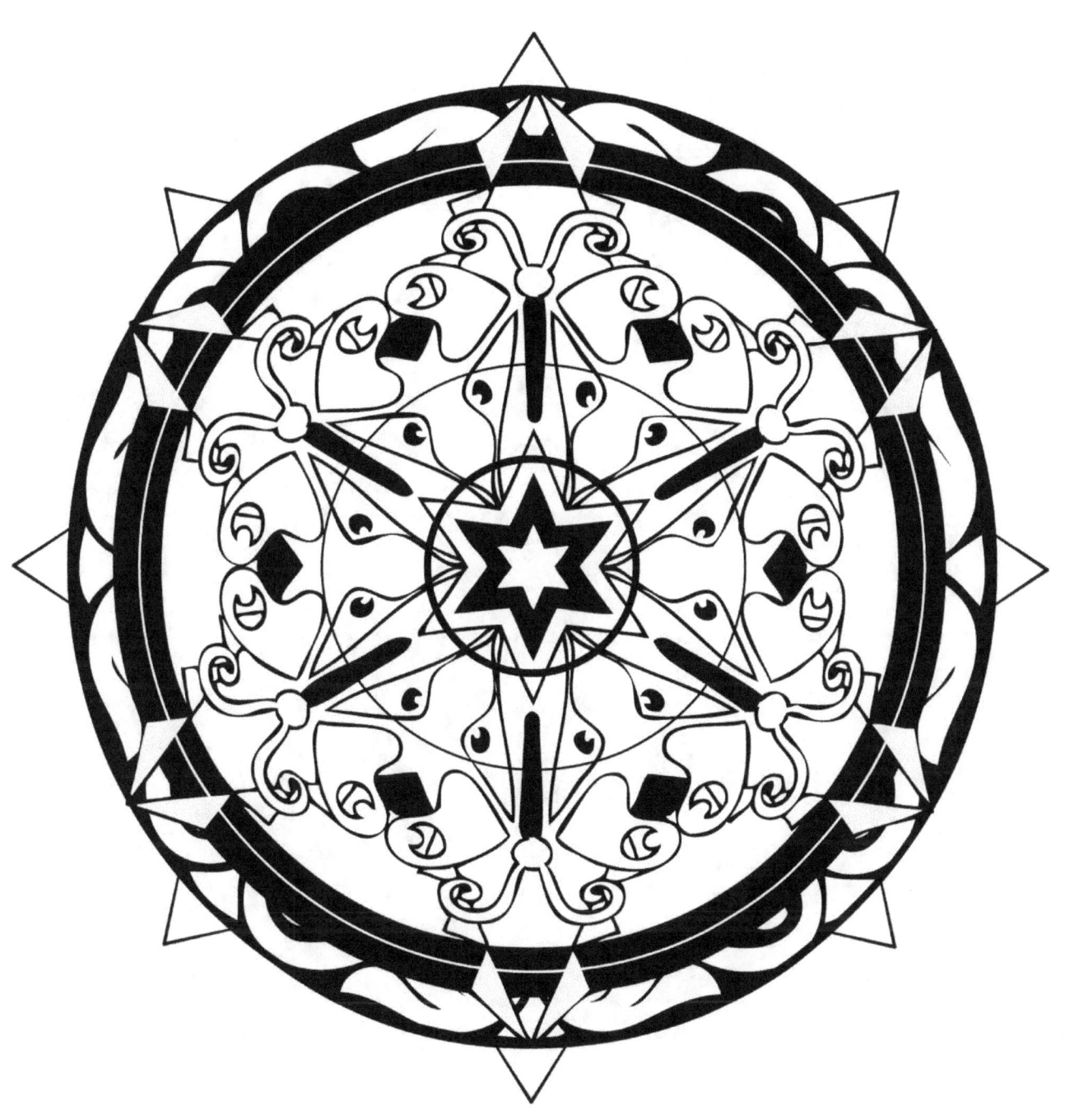

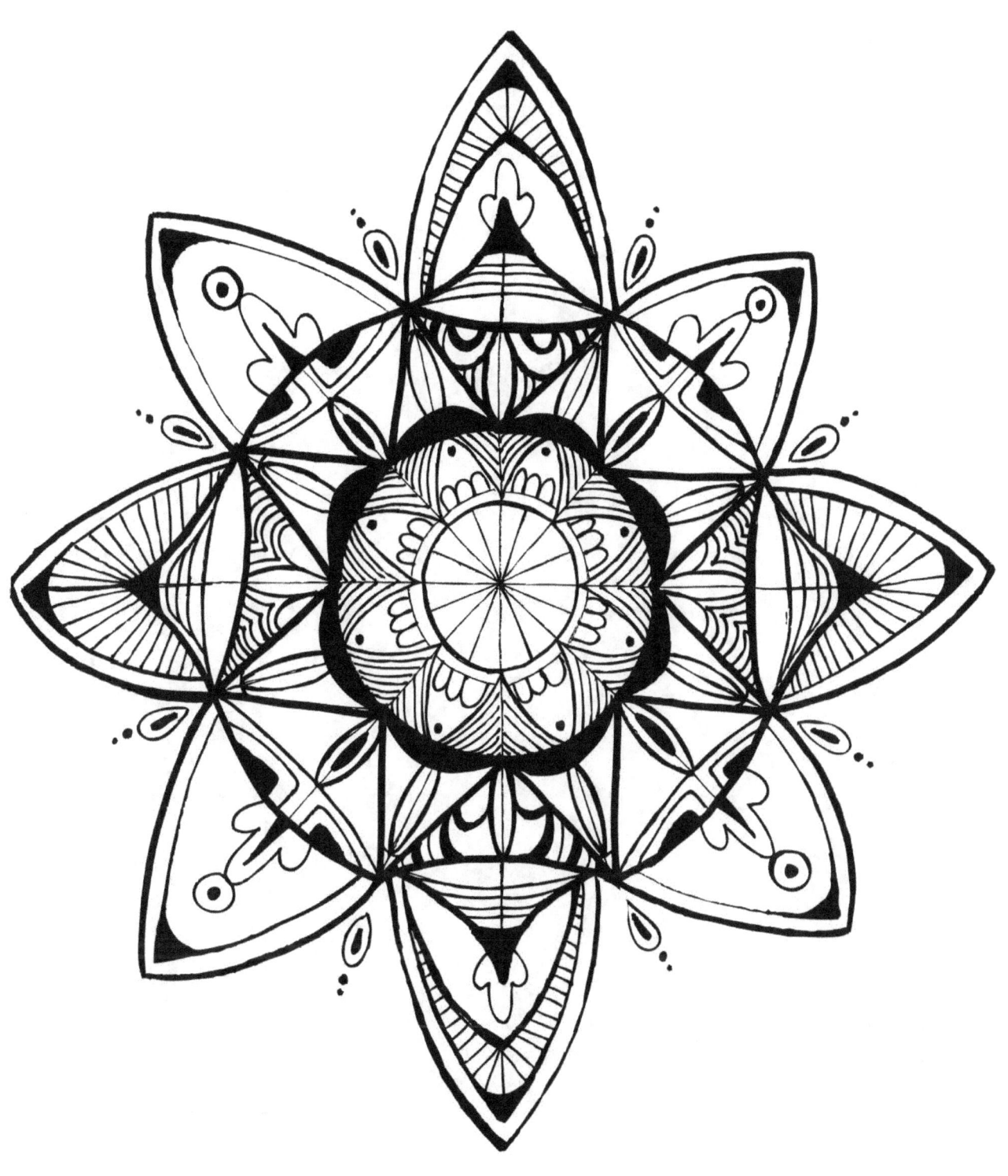

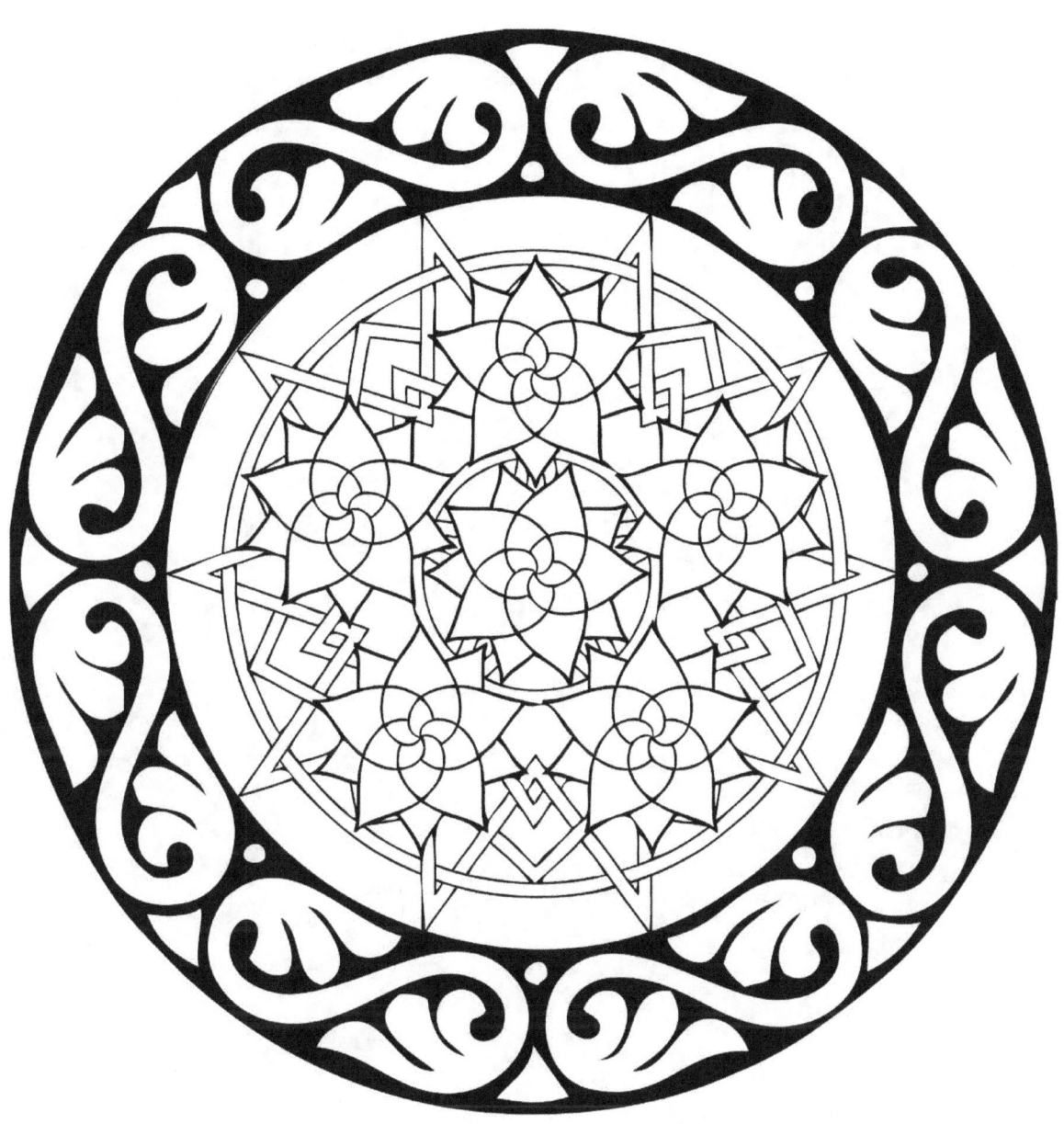

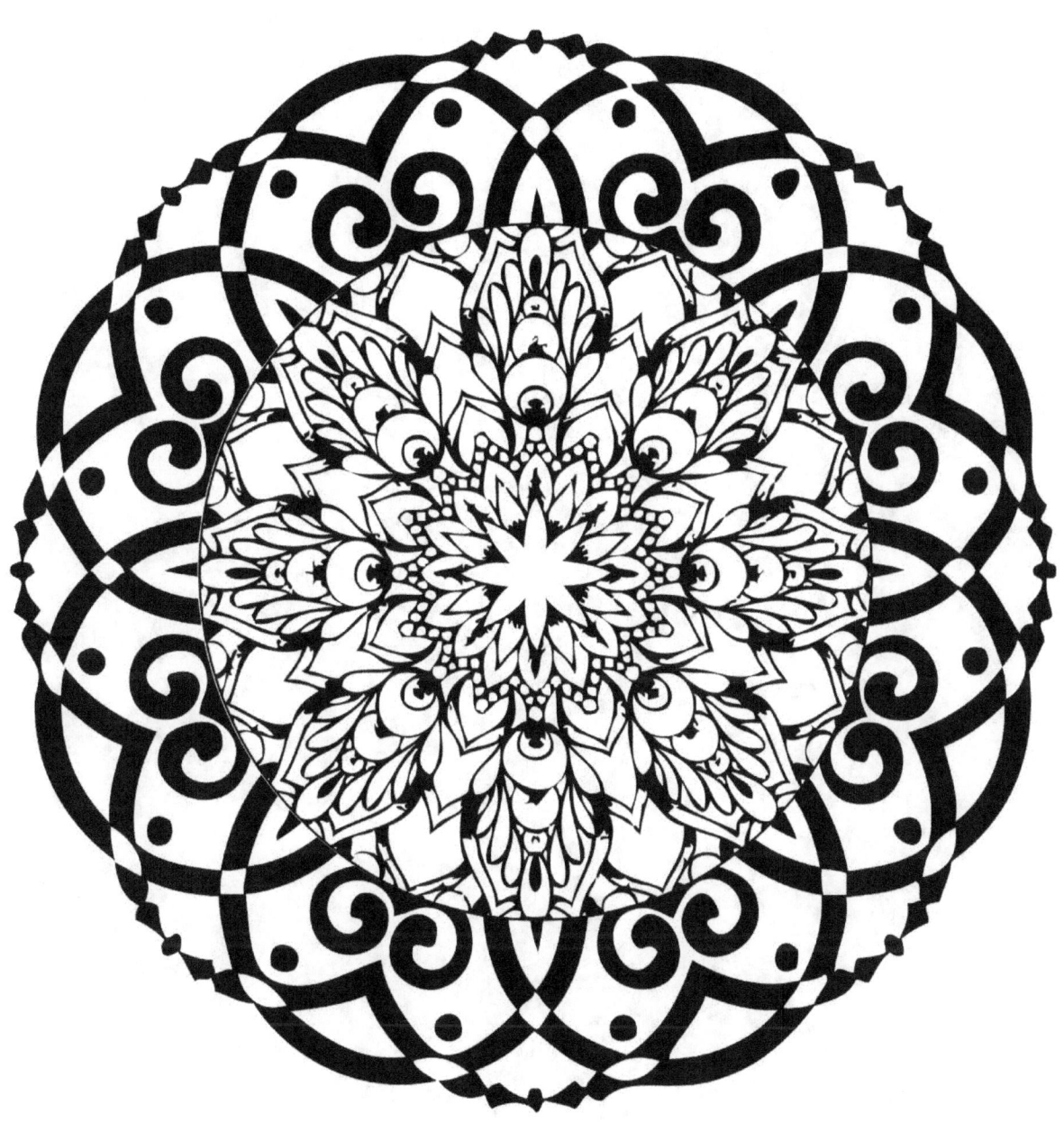

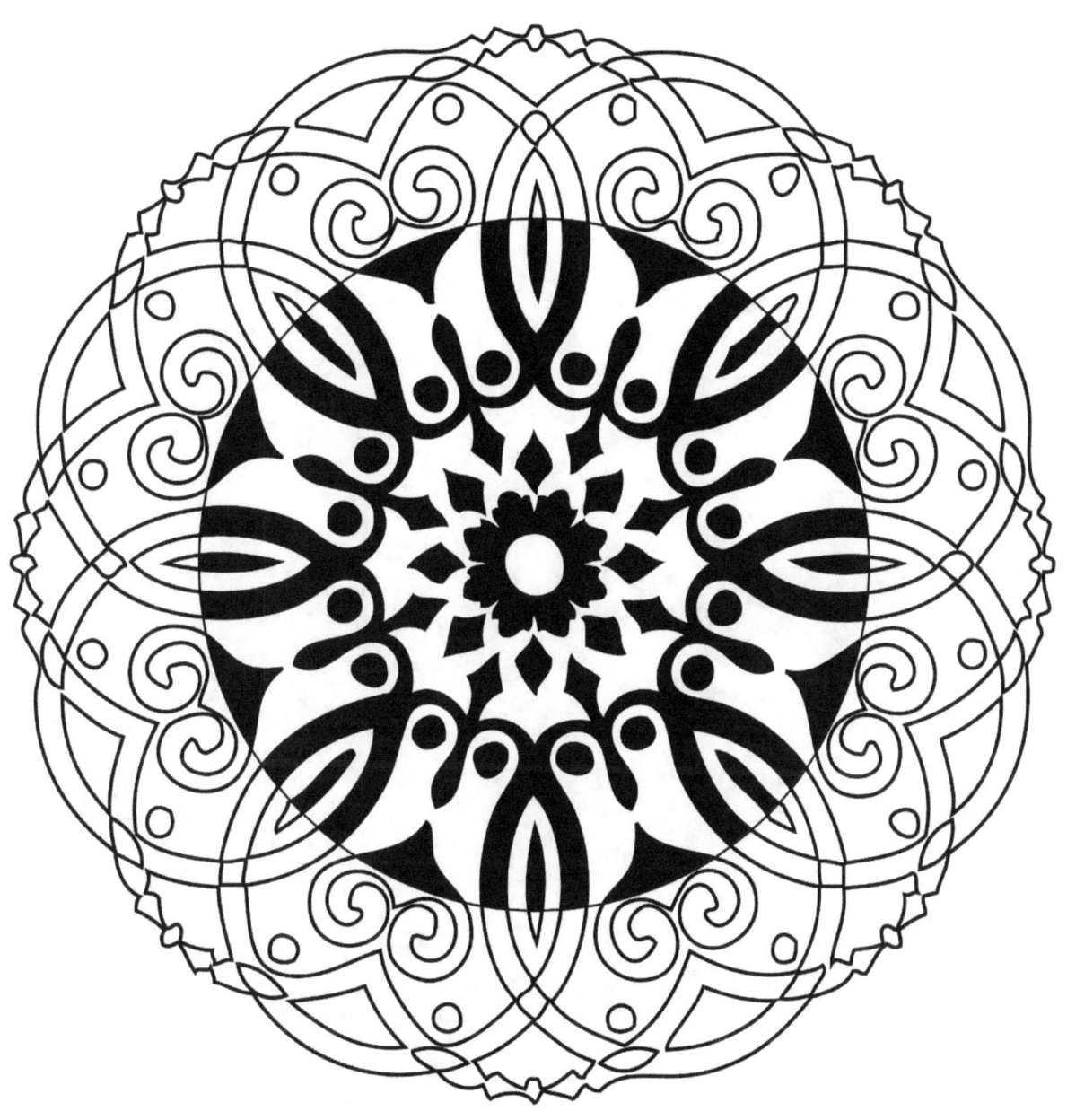

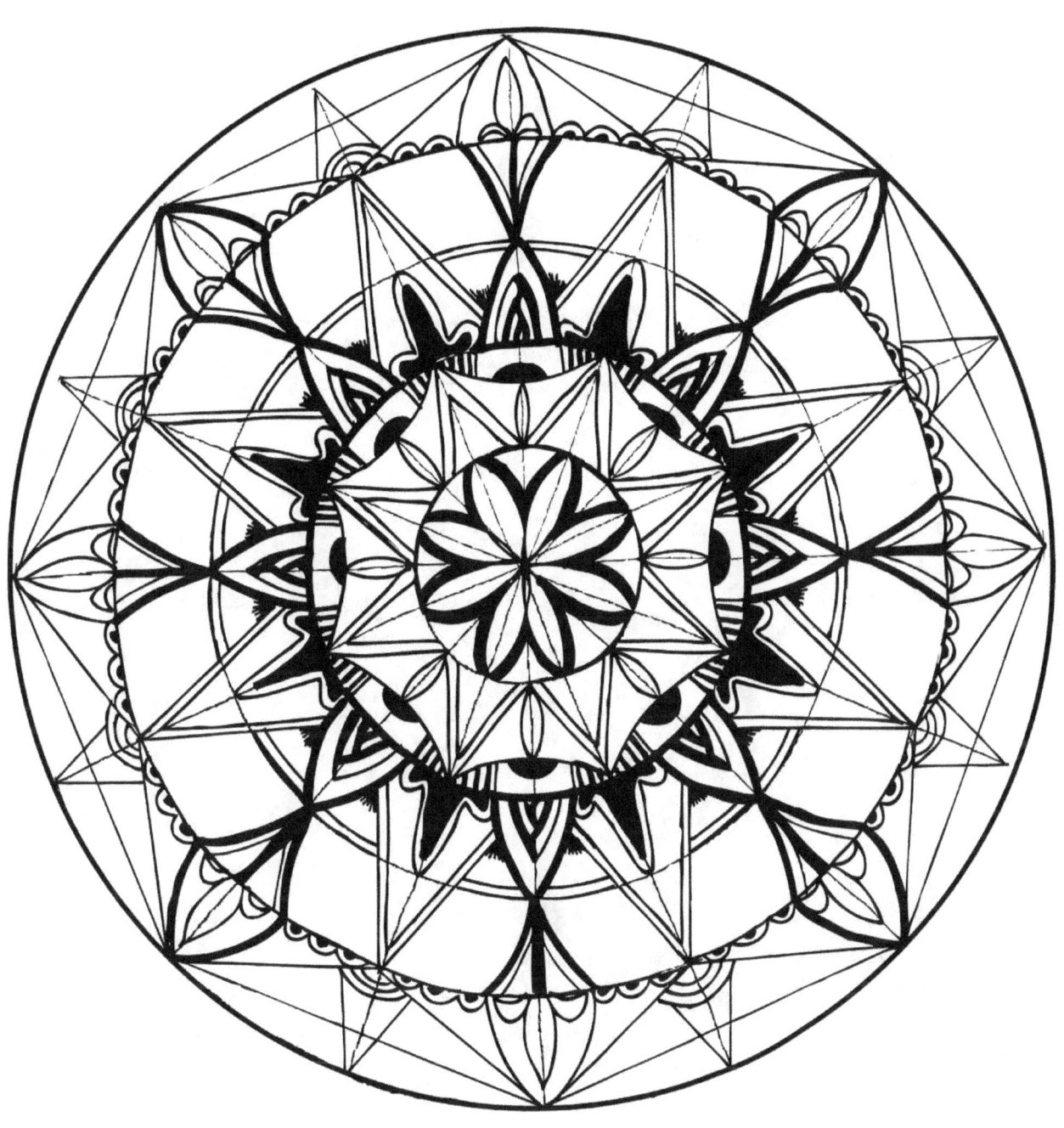

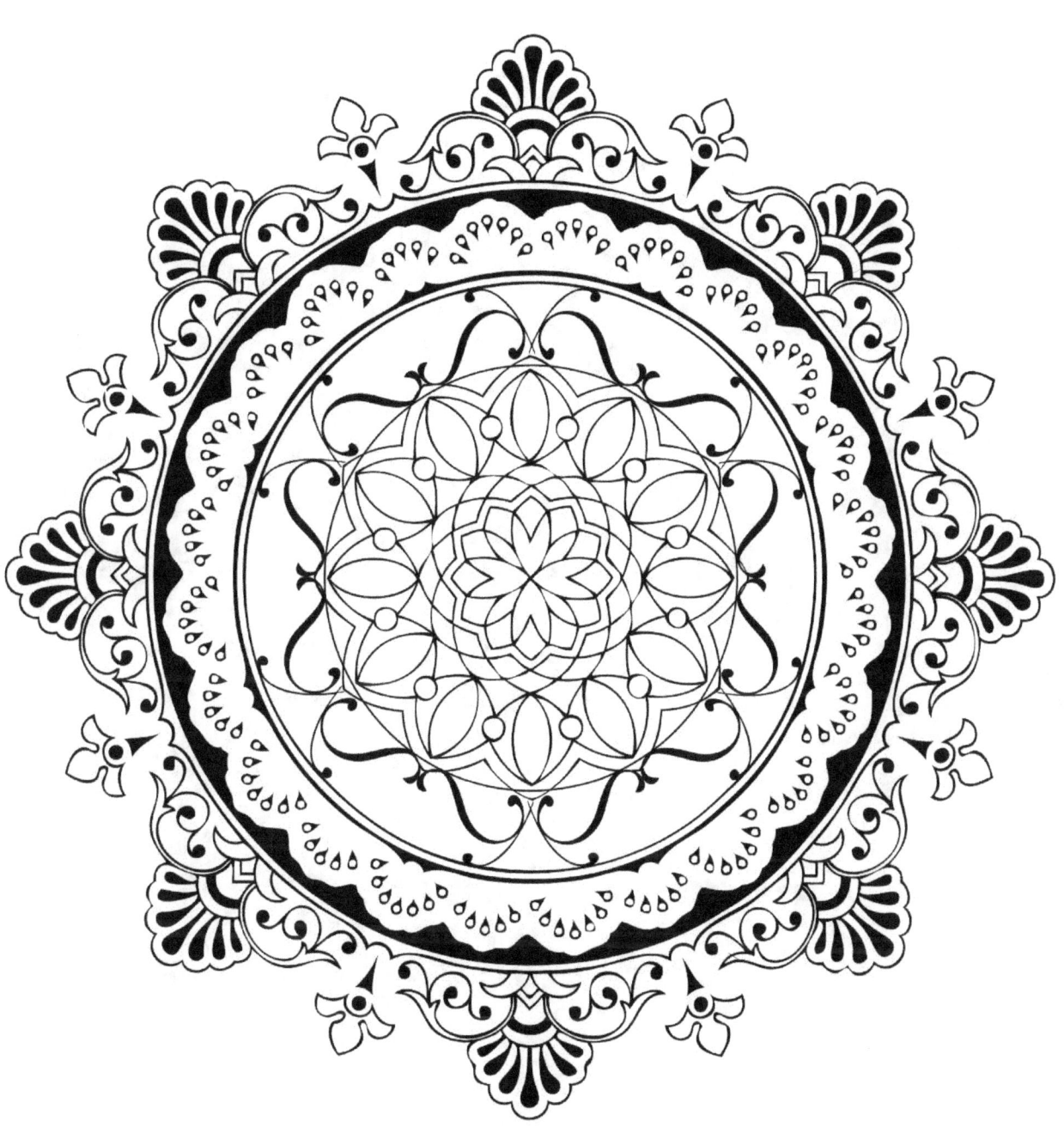

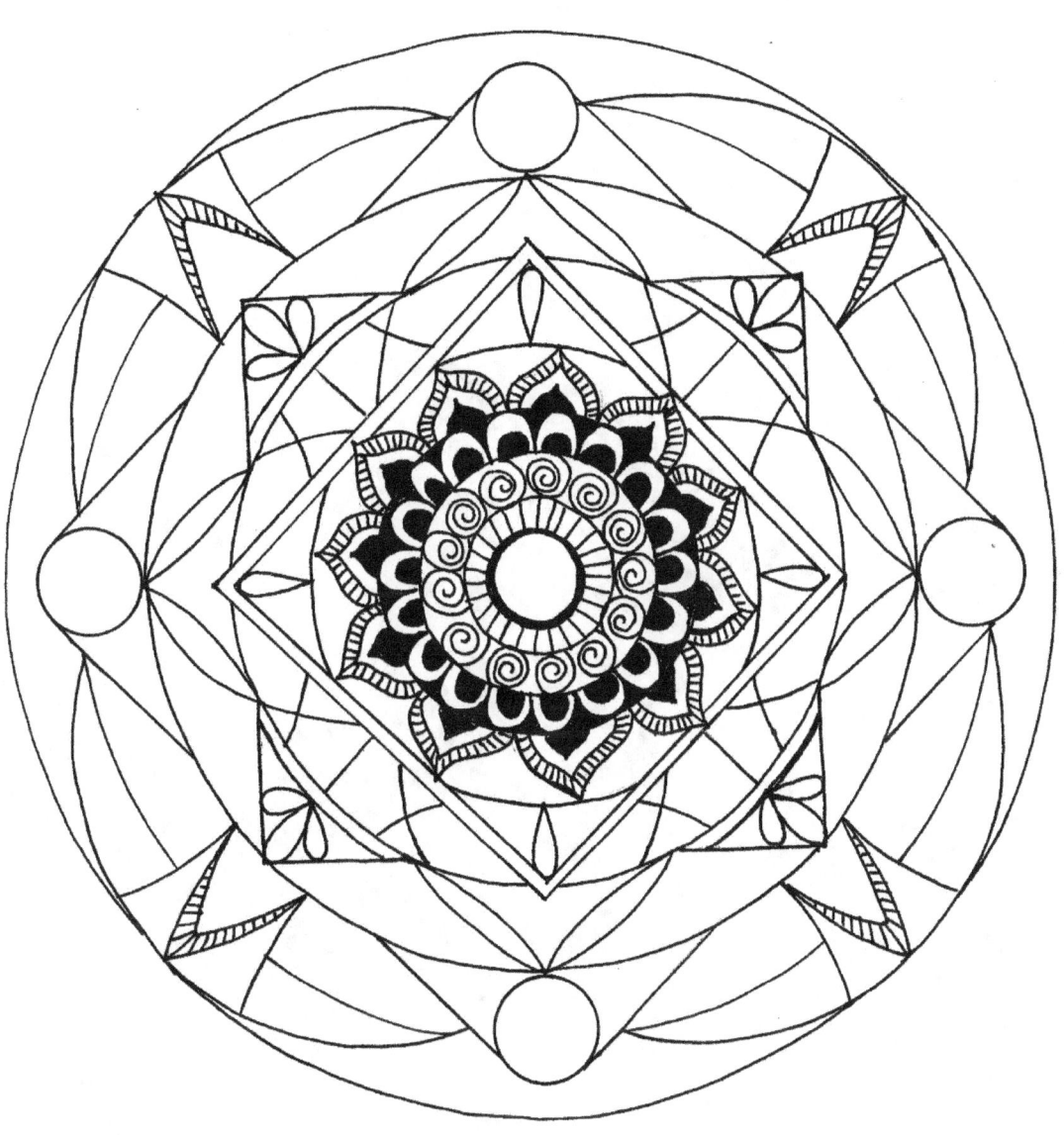

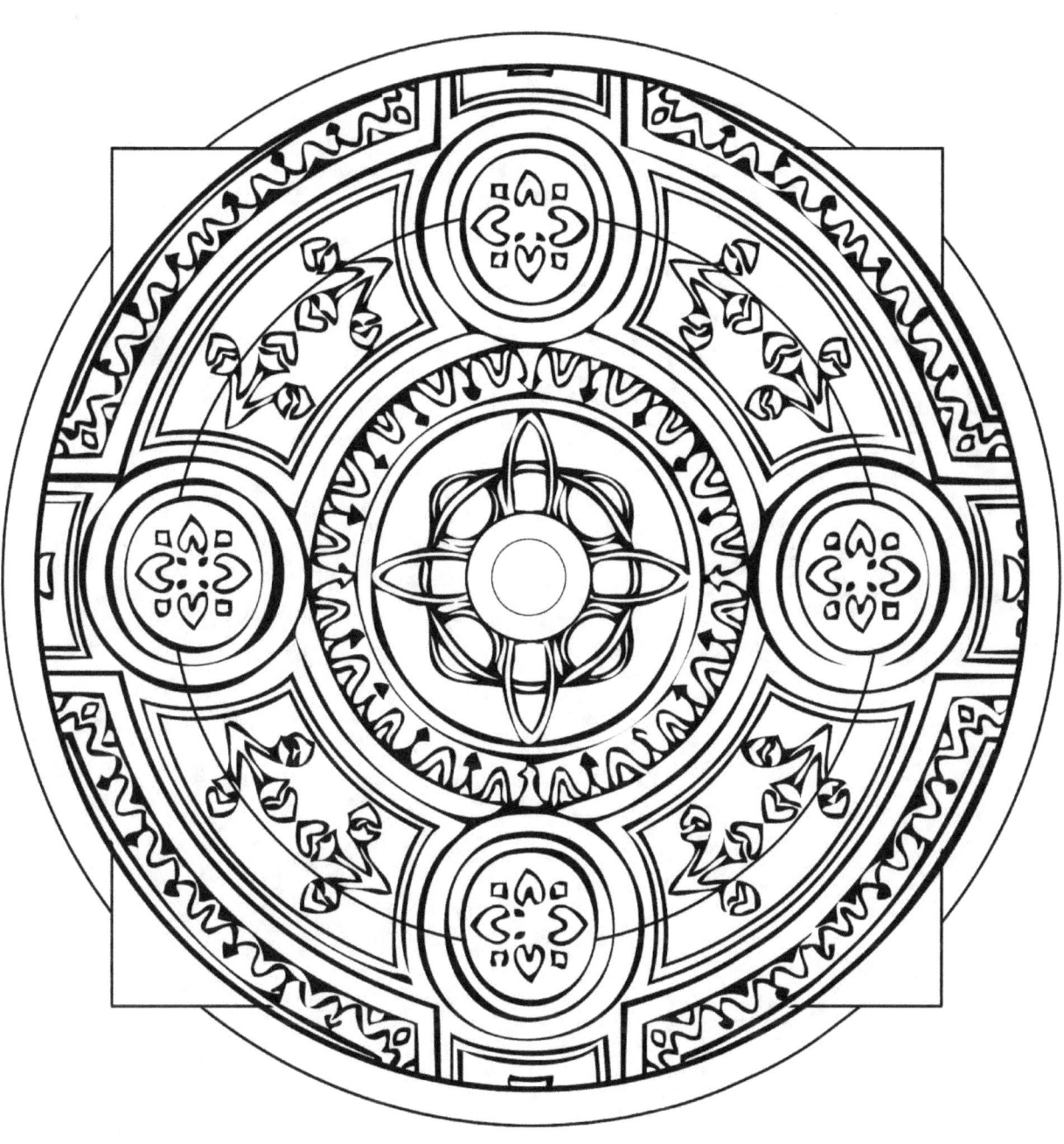

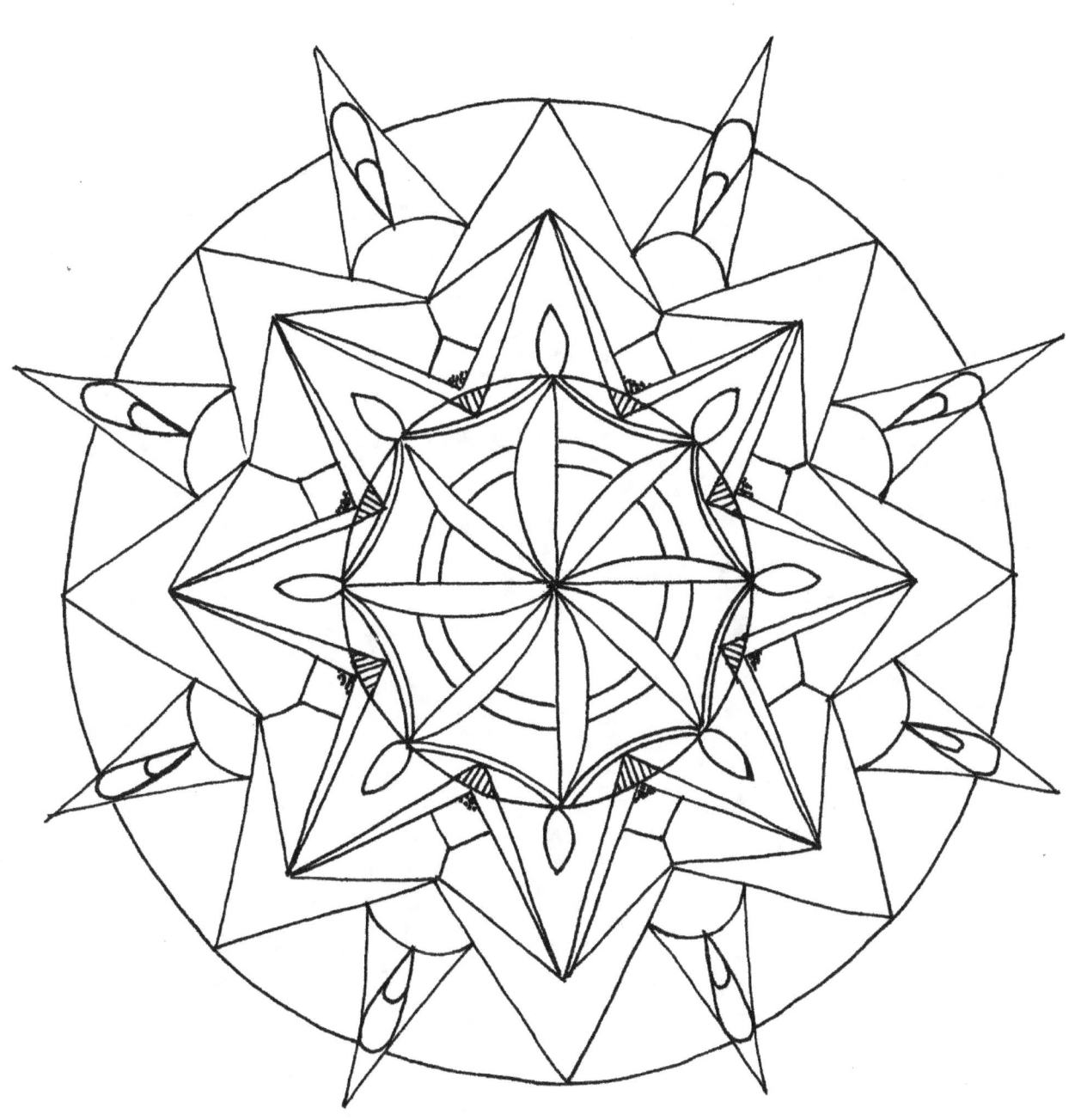

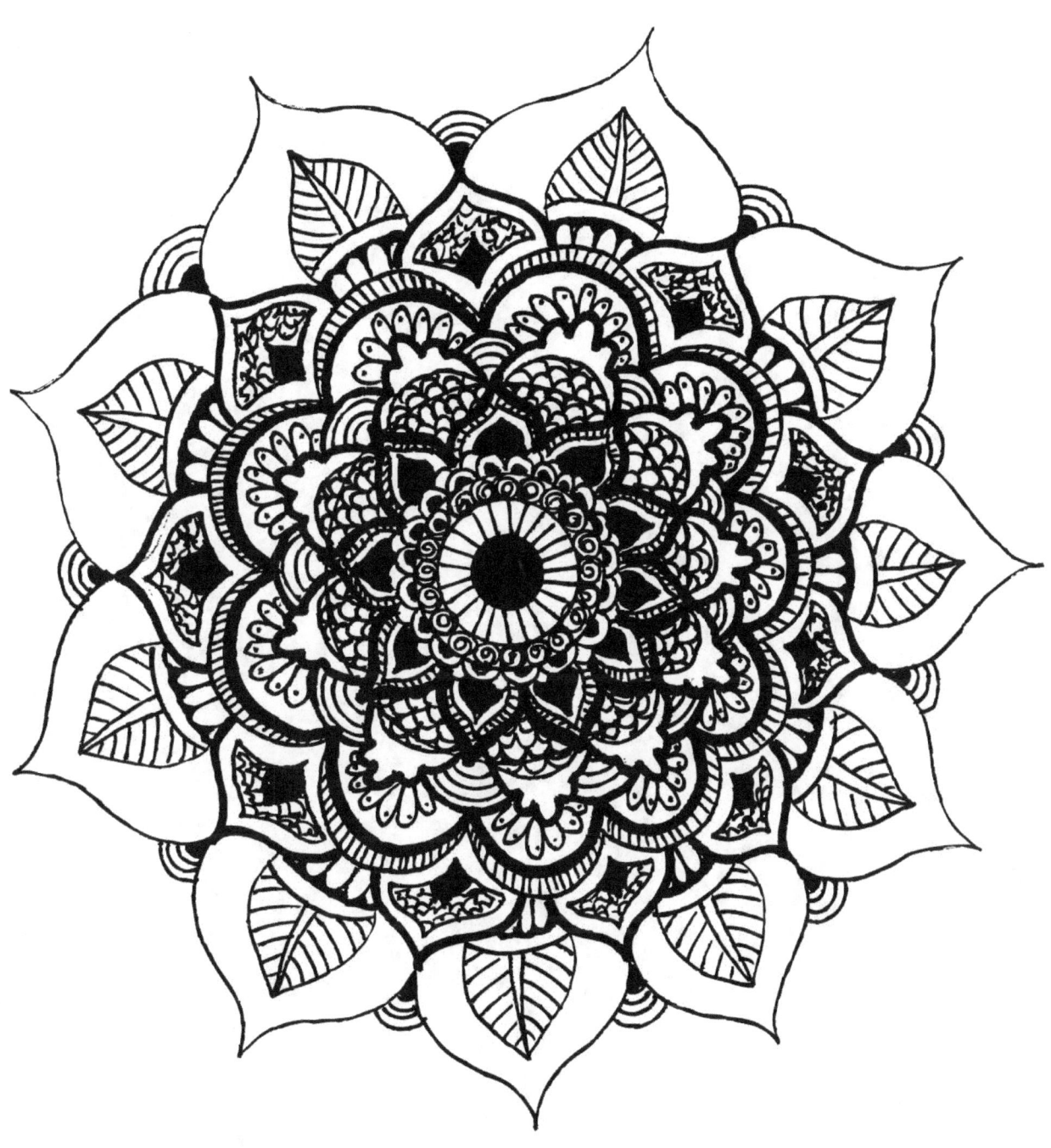

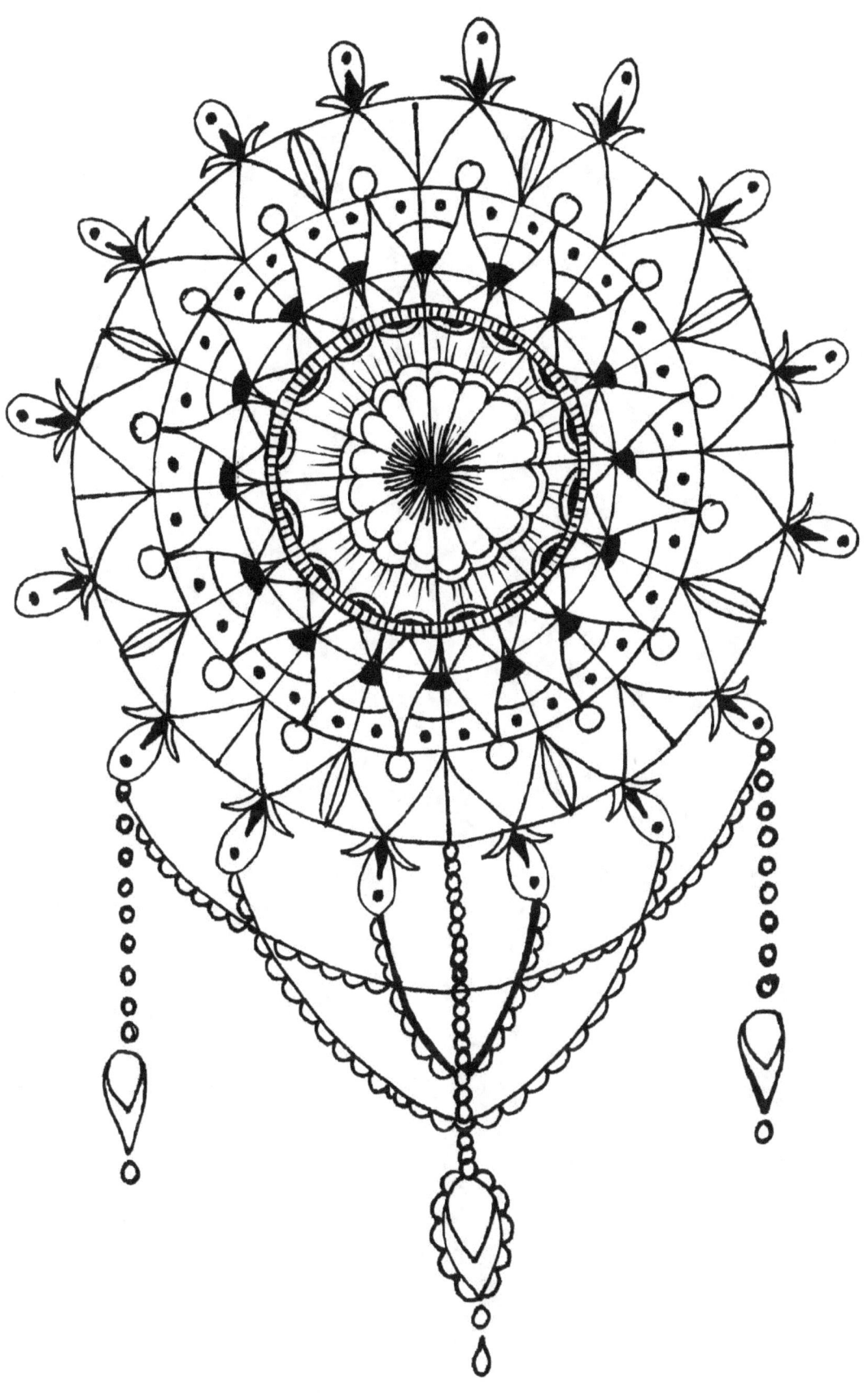

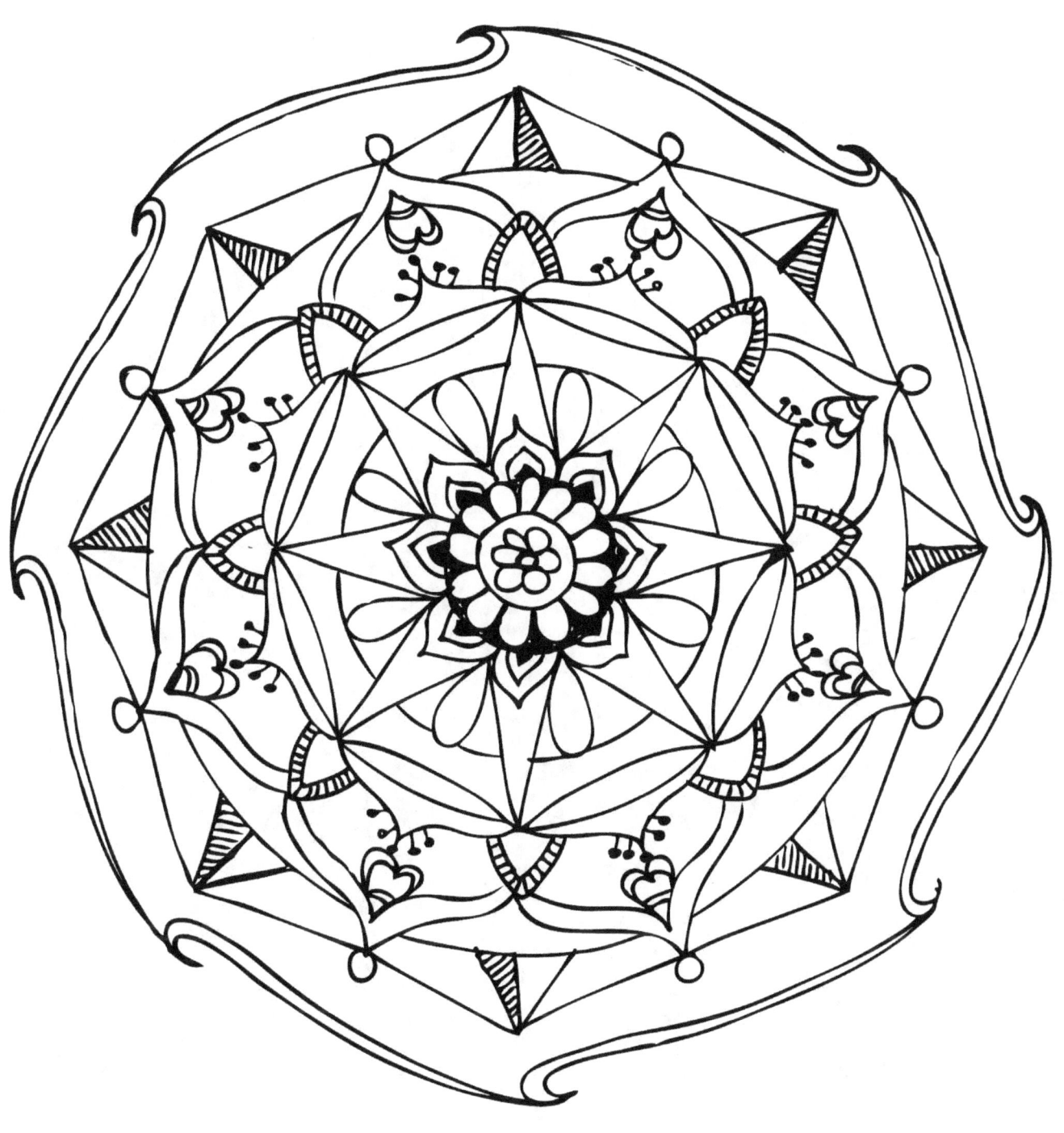